"I have known Dr. Wolmarans and his wife Jackie for a number of years, and have found them to be dear friends. I can recommend their fruitful ministry. He is responsible for many Bible schools and churches in Africa, Europe, and North America."
—*Freda Lindsay*
Co-founder, Christ For the Nations

"We have known Dr. Henry Wolmarans since he pastored his first church in South Africa. He did an absolutely incredible job birthing churches and Bible colleges. When you talk to him you realize the great anointing and the call God has on him."
—*Charles and Francis Hunter*

"I have known Dr. Wolmarans, both as a friend and a mentor, for ten years. He is an exciting teacher who shares a dynamic message. He has been faithful to use his God-given talents to birth churches, Bible colleges and schools, and various ministries, as well as author four books. Whatever Dr. Wolmarans puts his hand to, he will pursue with energy and devotion to Christ."
—*Randal L. Ross*
Senior Pastor, Calvary Church

"Dr. Henry Wolmarans is a distinguished, strong and successful Christian pastor and evangelical leader from South Africa who has made some valuable contributions for Christ. His focus has been to carry out God's number one job of spreading the gospel to 'every creature.'"
—*Dr. T.L. Osborn*
OSFO International

mw5xm5v24+

Your Rights
To
Riche$

Your Rights
To
Riche$

Dr. Henry Wolmarans

Tsaba House
Reedley, California

Cover design by Bookwrights Design
Interior Design by Pete Masterson, Aeonix Publishing Group
Senior Editor, Jodie Nazaroff

Publisher's Cataloging in Publication Data
(Provided by Quality Books, Inc.)

Wolmarans, Dr. Henry
    Your Rights to Riche$ / by Henry Wolmarans. -- 4th
rev. ed.
    p. cm.
    Includes index.
    Rev. ed. of: Enjoy financial security.
    LCCN 2003103805
    ISBN 0-9725486-9-6

    1. Finance, Personal--Religious aspects. 2. Wealth--
Biblical teaching. I. Wolmarans, Henry. Enjoy
financial security. II. Title. III. Title: Your rights
to riches.

HG179.W574 2003   322.024
                 QBI03-200439

Fourth Revised Edition: 2004

Published by:
Tsaba House Publishing
2252 12th Street
Reedley, California 93654
Visit our website at: www.TsabaHouse.com

Printed in the United States of America

Contents

Scripture Reference Guide

All quotes are from the New King James version of the Bible, unless otherwise stated.

Genesis 8:22	Psalms 35:27	Isaiah 48:17
Genesis 12:1-3	Psalms 41:1-2	Jeremiah 29:11 TLB
Genesis 13:2	Psalms 62: 10b	Joel 2:26
Genesis 14:18-20	Psalms 84:11b, 12	Haggai 1:5-6
Genesis 24:1	Psalms 112:1-3 AMP	Malachi 3:8-11
Genesis 24:34-35	Proverbs 3:9-10 AMP	Matthew 6:33
Genesis 26:1, 12-14	Proverbs 8:17-18	Matthew 23:23
Genesis 28:22b	Proverbs 8:20-21	Mark 4:18-19
Leviticus 27:31	Proverbs 10:4	Mark 8:36
Deuteronomy 8:7-13	Proverbs 10:22	Mark 10:17-30
Deuteronomy 8:17-18	Proverbs 11:28a	Mark 11:23
Deuteronomy 28:2	Proverbs 13:22	Mark 12:41-44
Deuteronomy 28:11-12	Proverbs 19:17	Luke 5:1-8
Deuteronomy 28:17-18	Proverbs 20:4	Luke 6:38
Deuteronomy 28:47-48	Proverbs 22:4	Luke 6:38 KJV
I Kings 2:3	Ecclesiastes 2:26a	Luke 12:13-21
I Kings 17:8-13	Ecclesiastes 5:10a	Luke 12:34
II Chronicles 20:20b	Ecclesiastes 5:18-19	Luke 15:21-24
II Chronicles 26:5b	Ecclesiastes 11:1	Luke 15:31
Job 27:13-17	Ecclesiastes 11:4 AMP	Luke 16:10-13
Job 36:11	Isaiah 1:19	Luke 17:10
Psalms 23:1	Isaiah 45:3	Acts 20:35

Foreword

Dr. Henry Wolmarans is, in my sincere opinion, a truly humble and anointed leader. I believe his ministry will touch and enrich any church or group where he ministers. In reading my friend's new book *Your Rights to Riches,* I was helped and inspired to better understand my rights. Dr. Henry has been used by God to help thousands of people. I know God will bless you with new thoughts from his book.

Dr. Oral Roberts
Oral Roberts University
Tulsa, Oklahoma

Dr. Wolmarans not only shows us God's plan for financial abundance he also challenges us to go for God's best and fulfill our maximum potential. This book will help you overcome financial pressure and experience the kind of freedom that God intends for your life.

You will begin to understand why financial success has been elusive to most people, and how to turn those circumstances around.

Casey Treat, Pastor
Christian Faith Center,
Seattle Washington

I heartily recommend Dr. Henry Wolmarans' book, *Your Rights to Riches.* It is written with freshness and enthusiasm that is contagious.

Henry Wolmarans, a distinguished, strong and successful Christian minister from South Africa, has captured God's perspective of material prosperity. He has presented this vital truth in a constructive and spiritual way in *Your Rights to Riches.*

If we expect to evangelize the world, God must be able to raise up enterprising, big-thinking Bible believers who will discover themselves as His co-workers and associates in business and in industry, in order to be the spiritual administrators of this world's monetary wealth for God's purpose.

Your Rights to Riches is presented by Rev. Henry Wolmarans for this purpose. It is a strong book and I heartily endorse it.

Dr. T. L. Osborn
OSFO International,
Tulsa, Oklahoma

Preface — A Note to the Reader

After studying the Word of God, I am convinced that God does not want the body of Christ to be decrepit, poverty stricken or poor. It is my desire to teach Christians how to come out of a life of financial stress and poverty into God's promised abundance.

Believers and unbelievers alike have maligned preachers throughout the ages, concerning their requests for finances. As a result, there has been little or no teaching given on this subject. Where there is no teaching, misunderstanding arises. Consequently, money and the church is a controversial issue. Teaching about this sensitive subject should therefore be without compromise, to avoid giving Satan an opportunity to bring strife and division.

You would think that people would get offended when you teach on money, but that is not the case. Demon spirits, religious spirits and miserly spirits get upset. Teach people the truth and no one will be upset, because when they know the truth, they will be set free from the satanic bondage of poverty.

During 1979, my wife, Jackie, and I took stock of our personal financial position, only to discover that we were broke. We sought God for help and He gave us these principles, which I will be sharing with you. They have been tested and proven, and they have worked in our life. I know they will work for you as well.

We were deep in debt and never earned enough to make it through each month. It would have taken us a year of our total income to pay off the debt, never mind money to live. There was no way out. Neither my university degrees nor my diplomatic career in London, were helping. So we began to meditate on, and apply, God's Word. We gave and believed our way out of debt in twelve months. We were able to buy our own home, a lovely car, and our income rose by over 500%. The principles contained in this book have worked for thousands of families.

Let me state emphatically that while I wholeheartedly believe it is the divine plan and will of God for His children to prosper, I do not believe that the teaching of prosperity is a "get-rich-quick" scheme.

God wants us, as believers, to feast in famine and reap in recession.

I believe this will be a turning point in your life. I am convinced that as we study God's promises concerning His plan for your finances, you will have a miraculous financial turn-about. You will escape from poverty into God's abundant supply.

This book will encourage you to believe for financial security by trusting in God's divine plan to prosper you. Do not misinterpret my intention by misplacing your trust in finances for security.

At this point, I will pray for you, the reader.

'Dear Heavenly Father, I pray that as this sincere person reads this book, the anointing which is upon it will be released into their life, and their understanding will be enlightened to Your will and plan for their life.

I ask that they experience a life-long, miraculous breakthrough in their finances, as they obey your Word. In Jesus' Name, let it be so, Amen."

—*Dr. Henry Wolmarans*

Acknowledgments

I would like to dedicate this book to the biggest giver per capita I know, the love of my life, my wife, Jackie Wolmarans.

I would also like to express my deepest thanks to Abby Ferrin for her assistance in editing and typing this book.

Chapter 1

Real Prosperity

My definition of true Biblical prosperity is, "Being able to meet your needs, and the needs of those around you, using God's power and resources."

Moses was a good example of a prosperous person. The children of Israel, in the desert, had no food or water. They did not even have the most basic necessities, yet God gave Moses the power to meet their needs.

A man, dying of cancer does not need a million dollars, he needs healing! You should be able to administer the divine power of God by laying your hands on him, cursing the disease in the Name of Jesus, and so, meet his need.

To be truly prosperous is to have your needs met, whatever they may be, and to know enough about the power of God to meet the needs of those around you.

Total Spectrum

If you restrict prosperity to purely financial terms, you are thinking of it in its lowest form. I want to give what I call the "Total Spectrum of Prosperity." It consists of five areas covering the entire spectrum of human existence. Please note their order of importance.

1. *Spiritual*
2. *Physical*
3. *Mental*
4. *Social*
5. *Financial*

1. Salvation

Salvation is spiritual prosperity. If you are not born again, you are lost. It does not matter how wealthy you are or how much money you have, if you are not saved, you are the poorest of all people. The most important thing for you to do is to make Jesus the Lord of your life. It really does not matter to anyone but your heir, how much wealth you accumulate on earth. What does matter is your personal relationship with God.

Let us establish this fact as the basic foundation on which we are building.

**Salvation is the most important
aspect of divine prosperity.**

2. Physical Healing

To have a healthy body is to be physically prosperous. As I have related, if you were dying of cancer, the most important thing for you at that time would be healing for your body.

A million dollars in the bank suddenly becomes worthless to you, if you know that you only have a few days or weeks left to live.

What would you give in exchange for good health?

**Jesus paid the price for us to be healed and to
walk in divine health,
for by His stripes we have been healed.**

3. Peace of Mind

Real peace of mind is only available to believers, because Jesus said in John 14:27, "My peace I give to you." This is mental prosperity. Unbelievers have no protections against the dominating forces of fear, oppression or depression. It would be difficult to verify, since medical science has not given an exact percentage, but many psychiatrists claim, "90% of all sickness is psychosomatic in origin."

We are referring to the soul realm, which incorporates the will, the intellect and the emotions. To be prosperous mentally would mean that you have control over your will, your emotions and your intellectual powers. If Satan can succeed in gaining control of your will, he will have a very destructive weapon in his power. Your will should be submitted to the Lord and used for the extension of the Kingdom of God. A controlled will, with peace of mind, would mean prosperity to many.

The key to mental prosperity is, renewing your mind through studying and meditating on God's Word.

4. Happy Marriage and Loving Family

When I say social prosperity, I mean a healthy, loving family relationship. There should be peace in the home! Understanding and acceptance by all members of the family unit, for each other, is essential.

Marriage and the family unit is the oldest institution known to man, it was established by God because He knows what we need. After all, He is our creator!

A healthy, loving home is the foundation for the balance and security in a child's life. Children are molded and shaped by their experience in the home; mom and dad form their character. A child's personality, strengths, weaknesses, attitude and values are formed largely by his family environment. A healthy, secure home atmosphere breeds a good self-image.

A good relationship between husband and wife is vital if they are to enjoy total prosperity. Behind every truly successful person is a love-centered, peaceful, well-balanced home and family. In this environment, jealousy and fear cannot survive.

Stable families breed stable and prosperous nations.

5. Financial Security

Last on the list is, financial prosperity or material wealth and power. It is both the lowest form of power and the lowest level of prosperity. The world places a much higher value on money, and attempts to get Christians to do the same.

Prayer is the highest form of power, because it enables you to release God's power. Money cannot buy health, salvation, love or happiness. It is not the highest level of prosperity. On the other hand, money is necessary to buy clothes, food, medicine, transportation, homes, education, military power, and even protection.

Money can be extremely useful, however, it is neither the beginning nor the end.

Benjamin Franklin said, "Money has never made a man happy yet, nor will it. There is nothing in its' nature to produce happiness. The more a man has, the more he wants. Instead of filling a vacuum, it makes one."

The World's Prosperity is Empty

Being a Christian is not a prerequisite to having material wealth, but it is for total prosperity, and financial security. The only way to enjoy true, sustained financial security is by serving and obeying God.

The first thing one needs to do is seek God's righteousness, and to be in right standing with Him. This is achieved through salvation. All the material things should then be added to you, unless you are being disobedient to the Word.

Secondly, lean on God's grace, His willingness to use His power and ability on our behalf without us earning or deserving it. Willingness should not be confused with ability. God is capable of doing anything. Grasping this is important, as it will give you boldness and courage to believe that God's grace has provided financial success and stability for you, His child.

Please do not forget the foundation we have laid as we progress to the heart of this book. Being born again will always take pre-eminence, therefore, I assume that my readers are re-born children of God. Having put everything into proper perspective, I now feel at liberty to concentrate on how to create and enjoy financial security from a Biblical perspective and with the proper motive of advancing God's kingdom on earth.

In summary, many Christians today instantly retract when they hear the word prosperity because of faulty representations and wrong motives by some teachers of the Word. Prosperity should not instantly conjure up negative feelings of the church grabbing for your wallet. Prosperity is much more than wealth and riches. Remember: real prosperity is achieved by using God's resources and promises to meet all your needs, as well as the needs of those around you.

The total spectrum of prosperity covers the five areas of human existence. Spiritual Prosperity is achieved through salvation. Physical Prosperity is being blessed with a whole and healthy body. Jesus has already paid the price for our health, and by His stripes we are healed. Peace of mind and protection from the dominating forces of fear, oppression, and depression are the third element, which is Mental Prosperity. The fourth, Social Prosperity, is essential and can be achieved through Biblically based, loving and healthy marriages and family relationships. The final element of prosperity is financial. Because this topic has been so widely misunderstood, I will focus on it for the remainder of the book. As you read, remember the foundation and perspective I have established in this first chapter. Financial Prosperity is only a fifth of the picture.

Chapter 2

How Important Is Money To You?

People have on occasion said to me, "Pastor Henry, money is not that important to me." Perhaps you have said it yourself? My reply was, "Perhaps you have never been really hungry or cold, and not had sufficient money to feed or clothe yourself."

If money is really not that important to you, give it all away to the poor, because it certainly is important to them. If you are truly against prosperity, why don't you move to India or Ethiopia where you can be poor in style? If you are honestly against financial success, why are you working so hard to obtain it? Resign your job and be poor!

The Biggest Need
The biggest need facing the church of the Lord Jesus Christ, in the next decade, will be to get out of debt and into a financially stable position. The world's financial system is in economic chaos and so are the majority of churches.

The greatest revival the world has ever seen is at the door. The Holy Spirit is about to sweep millions of people into the Kingdom of God. This revival will require millions of dollars to support and sustain it. If the Body of Christ is in debt, where will the money come from? With the collapse of the Communistic Empire, and the merging of East and West Germany, the need for finances to take the Gospel to these countries has begun. The doors are opening throughout Europe, and even China is more accessible now than at any other time in recent memory. Perhaps we are already too late, because the church is in debt!

Money Is Your Life

Normally one works 8-10 hours per day and is paid weekly or monthly. Money is a medium of exchange. Someone is effectively paying you to give him/her your life. Income thus spent to pay your bills, is actually costing you so many hours of your life. You are paying with days of your life. The car you drive, the house you live in, are all being paid for with your very life.

How you spend your money, is how you spend your life!

When you give to God, you are giving your very life. Now that is exciting! Every person who tithes works three days full-time each month for Jesus Christ as they give 10% of their monthly income.

The only way a Christian can really give his all to God is, firstly, by obedience to the Word in every respect, and then by giving financially.

Money Was Important To Jesus

Some say that money was not important to Jesus and therefore, we should not focus on it so much. However, upon close inspection of the Gospels, all the teachings on money, finances and prosperity, came from Jesus.

It is recorded in Mark 12:41-44 that on one occasion Jesus sat by the treasury, obviously counting how much each person gave in the offering. Suddenly He interrupted the entire service to preach about money because a widow had cast in one cent. He said the widow had given more than all the rich people as they had given out of their abundance, but she had given all she had. The true message of prosperity is not how much you give, but how much you keep.

In the book of Acts, there are only a few recorded quotations of Jesus. One of them says:

"It is more blessed to give than to receive."   Acts 20:35

If you were going to record anything Jesus said, why would you record that? It must have been important to Jesus and to the Holy Spirit, to make sure it went into the Book of Acts.

In Matthew 19:16, the rich young ruler approached Jesus and asked,

"What must I do to inherit eternal life?"

Jesus did not reply, 'This is what you need to do to get saved.' He preached a money message to him because He knew that this young man had placed too much value on his belongings.

How did Jesus afford a staff of 82 full-time preachers? He called 12 apostles, and later another 70, saying in Luke 10:1-4,

"Take neither staff nor coat [I will provide for you]."

Providing for 82 people on a full-time salary would have been impossible if He were operating on, what I call, a modern denominational Christian poverty budget.

In fact, Jesus had a large enough budget that He had to have a treasurer. Furthermore, the treasurer, Judas Iscariot, was stealing out of the moneybag and there was still enough money so that the other disciples did not even realize it was disappearing.

Jesus always had enough money to carry out his ministry. Whenever He needed more, God would provide. On one occasion Jesus sent Peter fishing to pay their taxes, not from the proceeds of the catch, but with the coin found in the fish's mouth! On earth Jesus was a prosperous evangelist, but in comparison to what He had in heaven, He was poor. Jesus deliberately exchanged what He had in heaven for a poorer life on earth in order to be our substitute, thus making His heavenly riches available to us.

I believe that in order for the church today to reach millions around the world, Christians need to realign their thinking on matters of money. The divine finances of the Almighty God will be necessary to accomplish this work. We need to realize that it takes money to win souls.

Let's face it folks. The world revolves around money. You work for a living because you need money to buy a house, food, clothes, to travel, and to enjoy your life. In order for the Gospel to reach the unsaved, the church needs to be financially able to provide for missionaries needs, travel costs, and supplies. You are the church, and you carry part of this responsibility.

As we follow the example of Jesus, we can recognize that an attitude of giving and sacrifice is extremely important to Him. He wants to see that our hearts really are His, that we trust Him to provide, and that we understand our part of the burden to finance the opportunity for the salvation of lost souls. To give all areas of your life, including finances, to Jesus is to experience a new level of wealth, true prosperity with no limits.

Chapter 3

Your Rights To Riches

In order to understand God's perspective on whether believers should live in poverty or abundance, we must examine the scriptures. God's Word is His revealed will. Knowing the will of God produces faith, without which it is impossible to please God or receive anything from Him.

Do not permit prior indoctrination or religious tradition, to cloud your interpretation of these scriptures. Tradition is the only thing that can strip the Word of its power. Jesus said of the Pharisees, in Matthew 15:6, that they had made the Word of God of no effect through their tradition. Allow the Holy Spirit to enlighten you as you study these scriptures with an open mind.

"Let them shout for joy, and be glad, who favor my righteous cause: And, let them say continually, 'Let the Lord be magnified, who has pleasure in the prosperity of His servant.'"   Psalm 35:27

God has pleasure in our prosperity, not in our poverty. While we are God's servants, we are also His children. If it gives God pleasure for His servants to prosper, how much more pleasure must it give Him to see His children prosper.

"The Lord is my shepherd; I shall NOT WANT ..." Psalm 23:1

I shall not want because the Lord is my Shepherd. God wants us to live without lack or want.

"No good thing will he withhold from those who walk uprightly. O
Lord of hosts, blessed is the man that trusts in You!"
Psalm 84:11b-12

Blessed is the man who trusts in God, not cursed! An upright man in
Biblical terms is a righteous man, which means he is born again and saved.
God said He would not withhold any good thing from such a person.

"He who did not spare His own Son, but delivered Him up for us all,
how shall He not with Him also freely give us all things."
Romans 8:32

God revealed Himself as the ultimate giver when He gave the ultimate sacrifice for us, Jesus, His only son. There is nothing you could
ask of God that He would be unwilling or unable to give you. You could
ask for your hearts desire, and provided your request is in line with the
Word, He will give it. You need not fear that your request would cause a
depression in heaven.

In the following scripture, wisdom is speaking. Allow me the latitude
to substitute "God" for "Wisdom, since God is Wisdom.

"I love those who love me (God); and those who seek me diligently
will find me. Riches and honor are with me, enduring riches and
righteousness."   *Proverbs 8:17-18*

Riches and honor are with whom? They are with GOD!
What are enduring riches? I would say they are spiritual riches. Money
does not endure. Inflation, recession and depression are all capable of
diminishing its value, the thief steals it and interest rates eat it up. No,
material riches do not endure, but spiritual riches do.

"My fruit is better than gold, yes than fine gold; and My revenue
than choice silver."   *Proverbs 8:19*

I will not argue with God. Spiritual riches are far better than earthly
riches there is no doubt about it. But we are not asked to forego earthly
riches to have spiritual riches!

"I traverse in the way of righteousness in the midst of the paths
of justice, (Why?) That I may cause those who love me to inherit
wealth, that I may fill their treasuries."   *Proverbs 8:20-21*

The Spirit of God is drawing a comparison between spiritual riches and material riches in order for us to correct our priorities. God provides for us here by instructing us on how to obtain wealth on earth, yet keep our focus on spiritual wealth. He is saying, "I will lead you in the way of righteousness so that you may inherit wealth." The following verses reveal God's plan:

> "But seek first the Kingdom of God and His righteousness, and all these things shall be added to you." *Matthew 6:33*

God's plan is to fill our treasuries, not empty them.

> "And all these blessings shall come on you, overtake you, because you obey the voice of the Lord your God." *Deuteronomy 28:2*

> "And the Lord will grant you plenty of goods, in the fruit of your body, in the increase of your livestock, and in the produce of your ground, in the land of which the Lord swore to your fathers to give you. The Lord will open to you His good treasure, the heavens to give the rain to your land in its season, and to bless all the work of your hand. You shall lend to many nations, but you shall not borrow." *Deuteronomy 28:11-12*

God is saying that because you are in the lending business, you shall not borrow because you will not have a need to borrow, rather, you will have enough to lend to many.

> "Here is what I have seen: It is good and fitting for one to eat and drink, and to enjoy, the good of all his labor in which he toils under the sun all the days of his life, which God gives him: for it is his heritage. As for every man to whom God has given riches and wealth, and given him power to eat of it, to receive his heritage and rejoice in his labor; this is the gift of God." *Ecclesiastes 5:18-19*

I can summarize what we have just read as: God-given power to enjoy God-given riches and wealth. In other words, He has given us the ability to work, the ability to earn, and the ability to enjoy what we earn.

> "I will give you the treasures of darkness and hidden riches of secret places..." *Isaiah 45:3*

The Bible is full of God's promises concerning His will to prosper us. Satan has used religious glasses to blind the church from their rightful inheritance on earth.

Jesus was God manifest in a human body. Everything He did was in obedience to the Father's instruction. He said in John 10:10: "I have come that you might have ..." He did not come so that you might go without, furthermore, " ...that you might have life." The Greek word for "life" used here, is Zoë.[1] It means life as God has it.

In Matthew 6:10, Jesus taught His disciples to pray:

"Your will be done on earth as it is in heaven ..."

Folks what is happening in heaven, is also God's will for the earth.

Paraphrased, what Jesus said in John 10:10 was, I have come that you might have God's life the way God has it. Streets of gold, pearly gates, health and happiness, I am talking about wealth that you cannot begin to comprehend. That is the way God has it.

God is preparing a mansion for you, not a shack! You are His son, you are His daughter, and you are a joint heir with Jesus Christ. You have a divine right and access to that. Isn't it interesting that we all count on having riches after this life, but feel that enjoying things now is a sin?

Jesus was our substitute for sin, sickness, and poverty. He became sin with our sin so that we could be made righteous with His righteousness. He became sick with our sicknesses so that we might be healed and walk in divine health. He became poor so that we, through His poverty, might be made rich.

"For you know the grace of our Lord Jesus Christ, that though He was rich, yet for your sakes He became poor, that you through His poverty might become rich."　　　　II Corinthians 8:9

As I pointed out earlier, grace is the unmerited, undeserved favor of God, or the willingness of God to get involved on your behalf. There are no doubts or questions as to whether God is able. However, there exists uncertainty about His willingness to bless. I often hear comments like "God is almighty, and if He wants to bless me He can." However, this scripture erases that uncertainty.

II Corinthians 8:9 does not guarantee you will be rich, but that you "might be rich." Although John 3:16 says,

"For God so loved the world that he gave His only begotten Son, that whoever believes in Him should not perish but have everlasting life."

---

1. Strong's *Exhaustive Concordance of the Bible, Greek Dictionary of the New Testament,* page 34, number 2222

Not everybody will be saved. If you reject Jesus you will go to hell, it's as simple as that. If you reject that it is the will of God to heal you, you will stay sick. If you reject that it is the will of God for you to escape from poverty, and enjoy financial security, you will stay poor. The same choice is extended to each of us in this scripture. Therefore, it depends on us whether or not we prosper, and not on God. Just as John 3:16 will only work for those who accept it, only those who accept II Corinthians 8:9, or any other scripture for that matter, will receive what God has given us access to.

People often argue that II Corinthians 8:9, refers to spiritual riches, meaning Jesus became spiritually poor so that we could be spiritually rich! While this did happen on the cross, this verse is not referring to our spiritual inheritance. If it were, it would mean that Jesus was spiritually poor during His earthly ministry! Does anyone really believe that Jesus healed the blind, raised the dead, walked on water and fed 5,000 people in a spiritually poor condition? If that is true, what should you be doing in the spiritually rich condition Christ provided for you? Jesus was never spiritually poor, except during His separation from the Father on the cross when He took our sins on Himself.

In fact, the Greek word for 'poor' used in this scripture is ptocheuo,[2] which means to be as poor as a beggar. The word 'RICH' (in contrast) is the word plouteo,[3] which means a full supply, abundance, rich in material goods. Let us examine other scriptures where this particular word is used.

> *"But those who desire to be rich fall into temptation and a snare, and into many foolish and harmful lusts which drown men in destruction and perdition."*   *I Timothy 6:9*

Opponents of Biblical prosperity and success love to quote I Timothy 6:9 as a scriptural warning against having material riches. Logical deduction reasons that if the word used here means materially rich, then it has to mean materially rich in II Corinthians 8:9 because it is the identical Greek word. You cannot spiritualize a word in one scripture and then materialize it in another, as it suits you. In order to retain scriptural integrity proper hermeneutic principles must be adhered to. Therefore, to infer that one Greek word has two meanings because you disagree with

---

2. Strong's *Exhaustive Concordance of the Bible, Greek Dictionary of the New Testament,* page 62, number 4433
3. Strong's *Exhaustive Concordance of the Bible, Greek Dictionary of the New Testament,* page 58, number 4147

,t produces, is spiritually immature. Interpreting scripture to suit
.trines is hermeneutic manipulation and borders on heresy.
he following scripture, some readers may want to spiritualize it
ng it refers to salvation. I do not agree.

The scripture says:

*"No man who believes in Him — who adheres to, relies on and trusts
in Him — will [ever] be put to shame or disappointed. [No one,]
for there is no distinction between Jew and Greek. The same Lord
is the Lord over all [of us] and He generously bestows His riches[4]
upon all who call upon Him [in faith]."*   Romans 10:11, 12 AMP

The word 'rich' or 'riches' is the same Greek word used in I Timothy
6:9 and II Corinthians 8:9. Jesus Christ generously bestows upon us His
riches, and He promises that we shall never be ashamed or disappointed.
It is a shame for a believer not to be able to pay his bills on time.

Believe this verse, as I do, and pray:

*'Lord, I have given, and your Word declares that I shall not be
ashamed. I put my trust in You.'*

God will never let you down.

As I revealed earlier, Jesus was not poor in heaven before He came
to earth. In relation to what He had in heaven, Jesus became as poor as a
beggar, born into the home of a carpenter, not one of royalty.

Jesus' apostle of love, John, also talks about Christians being prosperous. John, the only disciple believed to have died a natural death, was
eventually banished to the Island of Patmos after his tormentors could
not kill him. They even boiled him in oil, but he would not die. He was
an old, wise apostle when he wrote the book of Revelation, as well as the
following words in 3 John.

*"Beloved, I pray that you may prosper in all things and be in health—
just as your soul prospers."*   3 John 2

When he refers to his audience as "beloved" we know he is praying
for believers specifically. He prays that they prosper in every area of life,
which does include material things.

When he prays for believers to "be in health," he is recommending
living in divine health continuously. John goes one step further than

4. Strong's *Exhaustive Concordance of the Bible*, page 845; *Greek Dictionary of the New
Testament*, page 58, number 4147

receiving basic healing, by praying that believers live in divine health and simply not get sick.

"Just as your soul prospers," refers to the renewing of your mind. You cannot have divine prosperity or health until you renew your mind to the Word of God and start thinking God's way. This is the only way you can tap into the blessings of Almighty God, and prosper in direct proportion to the extent that your mind has been renewed.

"Beloved, do not imitate what is evil, but what is good."

3 John 11a

This wise old apostle said: "Do not imitate that which is evil." If John considered prosperity to be evil, he would not have directed us to prosper only nine verses before he makes this statement. John tells us not to do evil, and prays that we prosper, so one can conclude that it is not evil to prosper.

In summary, being a Christian and being financially prosperous are not mutually exclusive lifestyles. You can have both, and indeed, Jesus encourages us and teaches us how to have both. God has the ability to examine the intentions and motives of our hearts. He demands to be first priority, but nowhere does He say that means living in destitution and poverty.

He reveals our eternal existence when He talks about the mansions he is preparing for us in heaven, the streets made of gold, and the gates of pearl. Do you think that a God who understands the enjoyment of such things would expect us to grovel through life before we can live in luxury? The Bible tells us that we have a God-given power to enjoy God-given riches and wealth. Scripture after scripture speaks about not only an abundant future in heaven, but also the provisions God supplies on earth. He does not intend for His followers on earth to be unable to pay their bills and be shameful citizens. Now that I have Biblically established God's desire for you to succeed financially, read on to see what He requires of you to receive His abundant provision.

Chapter 4

Wealth Is Available To You

Riches are a direct result of obedience to God's Word. Abraham is a good example.

"Now the Lord had said to Abram: "Get out of your country, from your kindred and from your father's house, to a land that I will show you. I will make you a great nation, I will bless you and make your name great, and you shall be a blessing."

Genesis 12:1-2

It is one thing for God to bless you, but quite another for you to be a blessing. You cannot give unless you have something to give! Should you just have a smile or a warm embrace to give, you could be a blessing!

Remember when Peter and John were outside the gate of the temple called Beautiful, Peter said to the lame man,

"but such as I have, give I thee: In the name of Jesus Christ of Nazareth rise up and walk." *Acts 3:8 KJV*

Peter had healing in the Name of Jesus, to give to that man. You cannot bless poor people in need, if you don't have clothing, food, or finances to give them. Just a hug will not do much to improve their bleak status.

"I will bless those who bless you, and I will curse him who curses you, and in you all the families of the earth shall be blessed."

Genesis 12:3

Why were so many people to be blessed through Abraham? Because, according to Galatians 3:7, those that are Christ's are Abraham's seed. We are in Christ, and so the blessings of Abraham are also our blessings. That which God promised Abraham, He also promised the believer. We should expect to be blessed to the point that we are able to be a blessing. Look at what happened to Abram.

> *"Abram was very rich in livestock, in silver and in gold."*
>
> *Genesis 13:2*

Abram was not just rich, but he was very rich. Who had made him rich?

> *"Now Abraham was old, well advanced in age, and the Lord had blessed Abraham in all things."*   *Genesis 24:1*

It was God who blessed him!

> *"The Lord has blessed my master greatly, and he has become great; and He has given him flocks, and herds, and silver, and gold, male and female servants and camels and donkeys."*   *Genesis 24:35*

God said that He would bless Abram, and He did it. Abraham was obedient to God's Word, and God prospered him. Let us now examine some scriptures that promise prosperity to those who are obedient.

> *"And keep the charge of the Lord your God: to walk in His ways, to keep His statutes, His commandments, His judgments, and His testimonies, as it is written in the Law of Moses, that you may prosper in all that you do and wherever you turn."*   *I Kings 2:3*

If you are a doer of the Word, being obedient to everything that God tells you to do, the blessings of God will overtake you. Whatever you do and wherever you go, you will prosper. Conversely, disobedience produces poverty and lack.

> *"Because you did not serve the Lord your God with joy and gladness of heart, for the abundance of all things, therefore you shall serve your enemies, whom the Lord will send against you, in hunger, in thirst, in nakedness and in need of all things; and He will put a yoke of iron on your neck until He has destroyed you."*
>
> *Deuteronomy 28:47-48*

Notice, the abundance of all things comes from God. We ought to serve God with joy and excitement because of His provision. However, because many refuse to do that, as the previous scripture states, "they will serve their enemies." God, our Heavenly Father, wants us to enjoy His abundant provision, just as any earthly father wants his children to enjoy what he provides for them.

The first thing that comes to mind is that if I am disobedient, God is going to curse me. God is not doing the cursing. Hebrew scholars, say that the word used in the original Hebrew text is not the causative verb, but the permissive verb. This means that God is allowing it to happen, not causing it to happen. The reason it happened is that you walked out from under God's protection and straight into the curse of the broken law, where poverty, sickness and spiritual death reign. Be obedient and get back under God's umbrella of protection and blessing!

> *"If they obey and serve Him, they shall spend their days in prosperity and their years in pleasures."*   *Job 36:11*

"If" is a small but very significant word. The condition is, "if they obey and serve Him," and the reward, "they shall spend their days in prosperity and their years in pleasures." I believe that everyone wants to live day by day in prosperity and spend his/her years in pleasure. The key is obedience. Obey and serve Him.

> *"If you are willing and obedient, you shall eat the good of the land."*   *Isaiah 1:19*

There are those not willing to prosper, simply because they are not willing to be obedient. Others are not willing to prosper because they think prosperity will draw them away from God. However, prospering God's way could never cause you to turn from Him, as the prerequisite to Godly prosperity is to seek Him, and then to be willing and obedient. It would simply be an unbalanced life for you to eat the good of the land and be poverty-stricken in other areas. God wants you to eat the good of the land, wear the good of the land, and live in the good of the land. Why deprive yourself of enjoying the best, when clearly it is a reward for being obedient to God.

> *"Praise the Lord! — Hallelujah! Blessed — happy, fortunate [to be envied] — is the man who fears [reveres and worships] the Lord, who delights greatly in His commandments. His [spiritual] offspring shall be a mighty one upon earth; the generation of the upright shall be blessed. Prosperity and welfare are in his house, and his righteousness endures forever."*   *Psalm 112:1-3 AMP*

nce again, we have welfare, prosperity, and righteous-
t say, "Choose between righteousness and wealth." You
have both. We know we are righteous through Christ,
uld become prosperous as well.

he Lord your God, and you shall be established; believe
ets, and you shall prosper."   *2 Chronicles 20:20b*

The writings of the Old Testament are often referred to as "The Prophets." However, "His prophets" could also refer to men of God alive today
in the five-fold ministry. Believe God's Word and believe what the man
of God teaches, and you will prosper. God has called and anointed me
to teach this subject. I have prospered personally as a result of applying
these principles I am teaching. If you accept these teachings from God's
word, you will prosper just as I have.

"And as long as he sought the Lord, God made him prosper."
                                                2 Chronicles 26:5b

The Testimony of Frans Vermeulen and Susan Bezuidenhout

Frans Vermeulen and Susan Bezuidenhout appropriated these promises into their lives and have seen God's provision personally as
a result. They were engaged, and did not feel that they were in a
financial position to tithe. When they heard this teaching, they
realized that it was not optional to tithe and put God first by tithing a full 10%.

Within two months, they saw many needs met in all areas of
their lives, spiritually, physically, and financially. During that
time they were given furniture, jewelry, and cash with a total
value of $7,000.00.

Are you now convinced that seeking, serving, and obeying God should
bring prosperity to you? Even the most ardent protester must surely now
doubt his original views after such an overwhelming number of scriptures such as the following:

"... I have not seen the righteous forsaken, nor his descendants beg-
ging bread."   *Psalm 37:25b*

God promises that the righteous man will never be so poor that he
or his children would need to beg for bread. Wealth should cause one to

turn to God in praise, rather than turn away to the devil. Our thinking has been wrong. We have associated wealth with the devil's camp, when in fact it is a blessing of God, which belongs to the believer. We need to renew our minds to the truth that God wants us to prosper and enjoy financial abundance as promised in scripture.

> *"You shall eat in plenty and be satisfied, and praise the name of the Lord your God, Who has dealt wondrously with you; and my people shall never be put to shame."* Joel 2:26

We can conclude that God is not in favor of poverty. His plan is for His obedient children to enjoy material wealth and financial abundance. This is a blessing from God and not a trap of Satan, providing the receiver keeps his/her priorities in line with God's teachings.

In summary, obedience to God's Word is the key to tapping into your promised financial blessings. Remember, the more you are blessed with, the more you are able, and expected to, bless others with. When you place a limit on how much of God's provision you will accept, or expect, you short yourself and your ability to give to the Gospel.

Conversely, disobedience to God's commands produces poverty and lack. How then do we achieve obedience? The bare minimum requirement is that we tithe 10% of any income we receive, but foremost is obedience and openness to giving. I will further explore the principles and specifics of tithes and offerings in the following chapters. The premise on which it all rests is obedience and a willing heart.

Chapter 5

You Can Take This
to the Bank

I often hear believers quoting, praying and claiming:

"My God shall supply all my needs according to His riches in glory by Christ Jesus."   *Philippians 4:19*

But they have not planted the seed necessary to reap the harvest of this verse. The seeds they need to plant are found in the four verses that precede verse 19.

"Now you Philippians know also that in the beginning of the Gospel, when I departed from Macedonia, no church shared with me concerning giving and receiving, but you only. For even in Thessalonica you sent aid once and again for my necessities."
Philippians 4:15-16

Paul acknowledges that the Philippians were the only people who, from the beginning, sent money to help him spread the Gospel. He then goes on to write:

"Not that I seek the gift, but I seek the fruit that abounds to your account."   *Philippians 4:17*

Paul is saying, "I am not looking for a handout, I want you to benefit and prosper." I want you to have something in your account. I want a gift to come back to you, but unless you plant the seeds, you cannot get that return.

Compare this truth with the traditional thinking of Christians and unbelievers who say, "The church is always after my money." This is a lie from the devil, which has deceived them in their ignorance. They think this way because they have never understood the part they should play in spreading the Gospel. Until generosity becomes a natural part of your lifestyle, you will continue to misunderstand the prosperity message.

> *"Indeed I have all and abound. I am full, having received from Epaphroditus the things which were sent from you, a sweet-smelling aroma, an acceptable sacrifice, well pleasing to God."*
>
> *Philippians 4:18*

These Philippians had given sacrificially. But the Bible does not say that God loves a sacrificial giver! I have heard people say, "You must give until it hurts." God does not require that. God's love is not evoked once you become a "hurtful giver!" God loves a cheerful giver.

However, when you give, your gift should be something meanngful and worthwhile to you. Give your best and expect God to give you His best. While God does promise to supply all your needs according to His riches in glory, this promise is not a crutch for believers to sit at home and wait for riches to come to them. He expects certain actions that are necessary in order to reap the promised harvest. When Christ made salvation free, His intention was not for us to use that as justification for laziness. It is wrong and selfish to think, "Well, I am already saved, so why make any extra effort?"

To receive God's utmost blessings, you must give your utmost effort to applying His instructions. As you make generosity a part of your very nature by relinquishing control of your finances, you will no longer have to bear the burden of worrying about them. Can you imagine never having another financial worry? God promises to take care of the obedient giver. Trust Him to keep that promise.

Chapter 6

Don't Be A Slave To Riches, Let Riches Serve You

We will now examine some of the most profound statements about prosperity, spoken by Jesus.

"He who is faithful in what is least is faithful also in much; and he who is unjust in what is least is unjust also in much."

Luke 16:10

If you cannot be faithful in handling your finances now, you will never be given much to be faithful with. Jesus challenges one's character in this statement. If you will not give when you have little, you will not give when you have much. God will therefore not trust you with much.

Test yourself before God, and be ruthless about it. Are you doing all you can financially for the Gospel, or could you do more? Would God be able to welcome you into heaven with the words, "Well done, good and faithful servant."

If you are not giving now because you are waiting for your ship to come in, forget it! How can you expect a ship to come in when you've never sent one out? Start giving from your canoe, and your canoe will become a ship.

"Therefore if you have not been faithful in the unrighteous mammon, who will commit to your trust the true riches?"   *Luke 16:11 KJV*

Jesus is comparing the true riches with mammon. The true riches are undoubtedly spiritual riches. These are salvation, the baptism of the

Holy Spirit, the gifts of the Spirit, the anointing of God, etc. Jesus says that if you cannot be trusted with money, God will not commit to your trust the spiritual riches. Handling material wealth God's way is the acid test. Unfaithfulness here will prevent you from receiving the true spiritual riches.

Personally, I desire spiritual riches. I will never forsake the anointing of God for financial gain. One cannot buy the anointing and one cannot live without it! I would rather have glory than gold. Mercifully, He wants us to have both spiritual and material riches. Be faithful with money and God will entrust to you the true spiritual riches.

> *"And if you have not been faithful in what is another man's, who will give you what is your own."*   Luke 16:12

If you are not faithful with God's money by tithing and giving offerings, God is never going to give you your own money! It is a powerful statement that Jesus makes, but God demands your faithfulness with His money.

God also demands that you faithfully serve in the ministry of another person as a prerequisite to you having your own ministry. Jackie and I faithfully supported three ministries over a ten-year period with our presence and our finances. Two were new ministries just getting started. One is Family Harvest Church, which my brother Theo started, which has currently grown to 15,000 active members. Another is Pastor Ray McCauley's ministry, which has grown to 18,000 active members. As a result of following God's principles, we have enjoyed a prosperous ministry of our own for over twenty years.

> *"No servant can serve two masters; for either he will hate the one and love the other, or else he will be loyal to the one and despise the other. You cannot serve God and mammon (money)."*
>   Luke 16:13

Immediately everybody thinks, I cannot serve God as a rich person. I cannot serve God and have money. It does not say that! It says you cannot serve God and serve money. You can serve God and have money, as long as money serves you.

Are you serving your money or is your money serving you? This is an important question you need to answer. What is the relationship, and what power does your money have over you? If you do not handle money God's way, then you will become its servant. Have no love for it, but use it to serve you and the purpose for which God gave it to you. Money is supposed to be your servant!

Remember that you cannot increase in the power of God until you learn to handle money faithfully. What price are you prepared to pay to have the power of the Holy Spirit flowing through you? How desperate are you to obtain financial security God's way?

Inspect your financial situation closely. Would you invest in a company that made the decisions you do financially? If the answer is no, then how can you expect God to? When God blesses you, He is investing in His kingdom on earth. He is trusting, based on what He sees, that you will support the spread of the Gospel to every nation and person possible. Examine what changes need to be made in your spending habits, saving situation, and giving patterns, and make those changes! What are you waiting for?

God determines your ability to be a manager of the many gifts He gives, by the faithfulness you exhibit in your finances. Look around at those you know who are spiritually rich, and I can guarantee that their finances are in order, and that they are financing the growth of the Gospel through tithes and generous offerings. If you manage your finances in line with the Word of God, your money will serve you rather than control you. Understand its place and purpose, while keeping your focus constantly on the Lord as the supplier of that money.

Chapter 7

The Power To Create Wealth

The key to understanding why God desires you to prosper and enjoy His divine blessings is found in the following verses.

"For the Lord your God is bringing you into a good land, a land of brooks of water, of fountains and springs, that flow out of valleys and hills; a land of wheat and barley, of vines and fig trees and pomegranates, a land of olive oil and honey, a land in which you will eat bread without scarcity, in which you will lack nothing; a land whose stones are iron and out of whose hills you can dig copper. When you have eaten and are full, then you shall bless the Lord your God for the good land which He has given you. Beware that you do not forget the Lord your God by not keeping His commandments, His judgments, and His statutes, which I command you today, lest-when you have eaten and are full, and have built beautiful houses and dwell in them; and when your herds and your flocks multiply, your silver and your gold are multiplied..."
Deuteronomy 8:7-13

This is absolute abundance, without any lack or scarcity, and it was to occur in the Promised Land. As partakers of the new covenant, we are not in the Promised Land, but in a "land of promises." The moment a person is born again, they enter immediately into this land.

"Then you say in your heart, 'My power and the might of my hand have gained me this wealth.'"
Deuteronomy 8:17

Isn't it amazing that God blesses people to this degree, and instead of acknowledging God's hand and giving Him glory, they say, "I did it by my wisdom and effort"? Do not do that, but instead recognize God as your Source and Helper. Do not allow pride in your own ability to rob God of the honor due to Him.

The Key

"And you shall remember the Lord your God, for it is He who gives you power to get wealth, that He may establish His covenant which He swore to your fathers, as it is this day."

Deuteronomy 8:18

God gives us the power to get or create wealth, that He may establish His covenant. The power God gives us refers to the anointing of the Holy Spirit. He leads, guides and gives us inspired ideas on how to produce wealth.

This scripture gives us two reasons why God wants us to prosper. The first is that He desires to establish His covenant with us, which happens the moment we are born again. Even though the covenant between man and God existed prior to our new birth experience, it is not established with us until we receive Christ as Savior.

God had to prosper someone else so that the covenant could be established with you. It took money to get the message of salvation to your ears. God also wants to prosper you so that, through your giving, He can establish His covenant with others who have not yet been saved.

The second reason why God desires to bless you, financially, concerns His covenant promise to Abraham. He said,

"In you shall all nations of the earth be blessed..." *Genesis 22:18*

God is still responsible to fulfill this promise, hence the statement:

"...I will bless you and give you power to get wealth, so that I may establish my covenant which I gave to your fathers (Abraham) as it is this day." *Deuteronomy 8:18*

Remember, the heart of the Abrahamic Covenant stated in its simplest form is, "Abraham, believe me." Abraham replied, "I believe." It was counted to him as righteousness, and God made him very rich.

As born again Christians, we are Abraham's seed and heirs of his promise. We have access to the blessings of Abraham, one of which is definitely earthly riches.

The Cost of the Gospel

If water falls freely from heaven, why do we still have to pay a monthly bill to the local utility company? In reality it is not the water itself that we are paying for, but the plumbing that is laid in the streets to get the water to you.

In the same way, the Gospel is free, but it costs money for a place of worship, for vehicles, public address systems, audiovisual equipment and ministers' salaries, etc. It takes money to get the Gospel out!!

Through the wise investment of your finances in the Gospel, the Good News can be preached and multitudes reached for Jesus.

Salvation is a free gift, which cannot be bought at any price. However, I can assure you that someone paid financially for the salvation message to reach you. Some saints give of themselves, in tithes and offerings, to create a Gospel spreading environment. You did not have to pay for your salvation. Jesus paid the ultimate price, but somebody also had to finance your salvation! It did take money to get you saved.

We are privileged to be co-laborers with God as He reconciles the world to Himself. God provides the spiritual power and we give Him our life, which includes our financial substance.

Minister's Salary

A sensitive topic is the Pastor or Evangelist's salary, which should be recognized by believers as a significant part of the costs involved in spreading the Gospel.

Some congregations pray, "God, we will keep our pastor poor if you will keep him humble, so that he can be spiritual and give a good message each week." No man of God should lie on his face half of the week, believing God for his food or his clothes. He should be praying for the people, and believing God for an anointed Word to minister to them on Sunday. Shame on the congregation that does not adequately provide for and support their pastor. Scripture is very clear about a minister's salary.

"Do you not know that those who minister the Holy things eat of the things of the temple, and those who serve at the altar partake of the offerings of the altar? Even so the Lord has commanded that those who preach the Gospel should live from the Gospel."
I Corinthians 9:13-14

"Let him who is taught the word share in all good things with him who teaches." *Galatians 6:6*

The Levitical priests also took ten percent of the temple tithe for their own needs. While these scriptures should be sufficient to justify a minister's salary, for good measure let me add one more.

> *"Let the elders who rule well be counted worthy of double honor, especially those who labor in the word and doctrine. For the Scripture says, 'You shall not muzzle an ox while it treads out the grain' and 'the laborer is worthy of His wages.'"*   I Timothy 5:17-18

God is looking for someone to be a financial channel for Him. He needs finances to cover the cost of spreading the Gospel to the earth. To accomplish this task, God will give a willing, obedient, believer the power to create wealth.

How many thousands of ideas run through your head daily? If you are like me, you tire yourself because there are so many at times. Many of these ideas are God inspired ways to increase your profit, but an idea will never support you in its raw form, it must be acted upon.

So, why does God care so much for your financial prosperity? The answer is that it takes money to get people saved, just as it took money to get you saved. He sees believers as the key to establishing His covenant. We are co-laborers or employees, and just like with any job, there is a rigorous application process where you must prove yourself worthy of accomplishing the tasks required. He gives us the essential package to be successful, whether it is through the user's manual (the Bible), Holy Spirit inspired ideas, or through other opportunities He presents. Our burden is to learn to recognize them and take action.

It is also essential to change our mentality regarding the lifestyle of a minister or pastor. Would you put your money in a particular bank, if you saw the President driving a rusty old car? I sure wouldn't! Why then, would the lost want to become a part of something where the leader symbolizes poverty and lack? The leaders of our church should have the means to live in nice homes, wear nice clothes, and drive nice cars, as they are the visible representation of the church that non-believers look to. Granted, some ministers have gone overboard and only want to drive the very best car, wear the very best outfits, and live in the very best homes. There should be an internal moral governing that guides ministers to be moderate, yet blessed. God wants to prosper His flock, and the leaders of the flock as they faithfully spread the salvation message. We should not hold the minister to a different standard of living than we hold ourselves to. When we give our tithes and offerings, we must trust these men of God to disperse them wisely for the highest impact, which does include their livelihood.

Chapter 8

Money Is Not Evil

Is material wealth evil? Is money evil? Are riches a blessing from God or a trap from Satan? We must address these very important questions. We cannot say that material wealth and financial success is evil, because God is not wicked, yet is immensely wealthy. God claims possession of all the silver and the gold in the earth and of the cattle on a thousand hills.

Furthermore, in the New Jerusalem, the streets are made of pure gold and the walls are not made of rock and cement, but have twelve foundations of every kind of precious jewel. According to Revelation 21: 18-21, God has twelve gates to His new city, which are twelve feet high, and made of solid pearl.

Based on Haggai 2:8, all the wealth in the whole world belongs to Almighty God, so it cannot be wicked and evil to have riches. If being rich automatically meant that you were wicked, then God would not associate with rich people. Yet, the only friend of God mentioned in the Bible was Abraham, and he was very wealthy.

Satan is the Root of All Evil

One of the tactics Satan uses to discourage uninformed Christians from believing for financial blessings, is to try to persuade them that money is the root of all evil, which is absolutely not true!

"But those who desire to be rich fall into temptation and a snare, and into many foolish and harmful lusts which drown men in destruction

and perdition. For the love of money is a root of all kinds of evil,
for which some have strayed from the faith in their greediness, and
pierced themselves through with many sorrows."

I Timothy 6:9

Notice that the Bible does not say that "money is the root of all evil", but "the love of money is a root of all kinds of evil". You can love money without having a single cent, and often it is the poorest people who love money the most, as they need it the most.

Money itself is not wicked or harmful, however, one's attitude toward the money might be at fault. The same $100 that paid for the sin of prostitution, if dropped by a prostitute and picked up by a believer can be used to get the Good News to sinners and cleanse them through the crimson blood of Jesus.

People read: "Some have strayed from the faith...." and misinterpret the Bible as saying that riches will cause them to turn their backs on God. People who think like this are usually sincere Christians. However, the scripture clearly says that it is those who covet or lust after money, which stray from the faith. To lust is to have an uncontrolled, all-consuming desire, which is obviously wrong. You should not be lusting after money.

If you are coveting to be rich for the sake of having money, you are in error, and your motives are incorrect. Divine prosperity must be used to reach the lost world with the Gospel and to transform believers into disciples. If you want wealth to consume on your own lusts, you will stray from the faith in your attempt to obtain it.

Money does not possess inherent evil powers. It is what you do with it, or your attitude toward it, which makes it potentially evil. God is not against His children being rich, but definitely objects to them being covetous.

Material wealth could not be evil if God has given us the power to create it. Remember that while God wants us to enjoy divine abundance, He demands that we be channels through which He can meet the needs of others and extend His kingdom.

In summary, money is not the "root of all evil," Satan is. The possession of material wealth and riches does not disqualify a person from being a Christian. A love of money could hold you back from the kingdom of heaven, but often it is the rich people who have this problem, because they see money as the answer to their problems rather than God.

Every person should examine their motives when it comes to money, to ensure that they are not lusting or coveting after money or riches. Money is put into the hands of faithful believers with the primary purpose of making it possible for God to extend His kingdom. A daily focus on Him will assist believers in keeping pure motives when they are blessed with abundance.

Chapter 9

Your Personal Financial Plan

Many people who have applied the principles contained in this book are now debt free. Some people have also paid off their homes, and others have doubled or even tripled their annual income.

God's financial plan will do two things simultaneously:

A) It will enable the Gospel to be preached throughout the whole world so that multitudes may be saved and grow to maturity.

B) It will cause you to prosper and become financially secure.

In order to enjoy the benefits of God's financial system, one must give tithes and offerings.

It is recorded in the book of Acts that an angel visited a man called Cornelius. He was an extremely generous man who also prayed consistently. The angel said to him:

> *"Your prayers and your giving have come up before God as a memorial."*
> Acts 10:4

The word "memorial", according to Webster's Dictionary, is something designed to perpetuate remembrance of a person. In Exodus 17:14 Moses was told to make a "book of remembrance" as a record or memorial for Joshua. Your giving keeps the memory of you alive with God. God takes as much cognizance of your giving as He does of your prayers.

We are going to do an in-depth study of tithing. It's on this foundation that you will be able to build a life of financial security, and is a critical element of this book.

Say "Thank You" by Tithing

Have you ever wanted to say, "thank you", or show your appreciation for what God has done? When our prayers are answered, it doesn't seem like enough to just say, "Thank you, Lord". Tithing is certainly a way of saying thank you, because you are giving back a little of what God has blessed you with.

You Have a Financial Responsibility to Tithe

What are you doing about financing someone else's salvation? Are you doing more for God this year than you did last year, or are you doing less because, financially, things have tightened up?

If the ministry you belong to had closed last year because of a lack of finances, how many people would have missed the opportunity of being saved from a Christ-less eternity? As I said earlier, you owe your salvation to some faithful believers who were tithing.

Consider the losses should your ministry close down at the end of this month. Thousands of people would go to hell because of your absence. God has placed you there to harvest that field. Almighty God is depending on you to finance the revival in your corner of the world. Realize and accept the responsibility that goes with prosperity.

Gross or Net?

Someone once asked me, "Should I tithe on my gross or my net income?" The usual deductions that are made from your gross income are, pension fund, medical insurance, and taxes. All of these are for your benefit. Even taxes are for your country to provide amenities for you. Therefore, my answer is:

Tithe on your gross income.

When you tithe on your gross income, you get God involved in your taxes.

"Tell us, therefore, what do You think? Is it lawful to pay taxes to Caesar, or not? But Jesus perceived their wickedness, and said,

'Why do you test me, you hypocrites? Show Me the tax money.'
So they brought Him a denarius [one day's wage]. And He said
to them, 'Whose image and inscription is this?' They said to Him,
Caesar's. And He said to them, 'Render therefore to Caesar the
things that are Caesar's and to God the things that are God's.'"

Matthew 22:17-21

If you "render to Caesar what is Caesar's" (or the government) before you tithe, then you are giving to "Caesar" before you are giving to God. You are putting your government above God.

The Practice of Tithing Commenced Before the Law of Moses

Abram paid the first recorded tithe in the Bible to Melchizadek, who is symbolic of Jesus Christ.

"Then Melchizadek King of Salem brought out bread and wine;
he was the priest of God Most High. And he blessed him and said,
'Blessed be Abram of God Most High, possessor of heaven and earth;
And blessed be God Most High, who has delivered your enemies
into your hand.' And He gave Him a tithe of all."

Genesis 14:18-20

This incident of tithing occurred some 430 years before the Law of Moses was introduced. Even though tithing was also part of the Mosaic Law so that the Levitical priesthood could be supported fulltime, we are first introduced to the tithe in Genesis with Abram. Abram must have been instructed by God to tithe, otherwise how would he have known to do it? The God-given instruction on tithing was never limited to the law, nor did God ever intend it to be. We will study tithing in the New Testament a little further on in this chapter.

A tithe represents ten percent (10%) or one-tenth of all your income. Jacob also made a vow to tithe, not because of any commitment to a law, but out of appreciation for God.

"And of all that you give me I will surely give a tenth to you."

Genesis 28:22b

The Bible teaches that we should tithe from our capital and assets, and not only from our monthly income. This may be a hard pill for some to swallow, but it is scriptural. When you sell your home, business, shares, or liquidate investments; you ought to tithe on the capital gain you have made.

"Honor the Lord with your capital and sufficiency [from righteous labors] and with the first-fruits of all your income; So shall your storage places be filled with plenty, and your vats shall be overflowing with new wine!"   Proverbs 3:9-10 AMP

This passage tells believers to tithe from the first fruits of all income, not only a portion chosen to take into account. If you disagree with this you are telling God that everything you own does not belong to Him.

By withholding your assets,
you set a limit on your commitment to God.

You have to make a decision. Either you are in covenant with God, in which case all that you have belongs to God and all that He has belongs to you, or you are not!

In Luke 16:11, Jesus said,

"Therefore if you have not been faithful in the unrighteous mammon who will commit to your trust the true riches."

Or, in my paraphrase, "If you cannot be trusted with the unrighteous mammon, who will trust you with the true riches."

Christians, who are disobedient and not trustworthy in the handling of God's tithe, will not enjoy an overflowing of the New Wine. New Wine is symbolic of the Holy Spirit throughout the scriptures.

If you want your storage place to be filled with plenty, and to enjoy a continuous abundant supply, then it is imperative that you tithe from your assets, capital and all your income. Now that you have this knowledge, you will be held responsible to live according to this truth. Remember, obedience is better than sacrifice:

"Has the Lord as great delight in burnt offerings and sacrifices, as in obeying the voice of the Lord? Behold, to obey is better than sacrifice, and to heed than the fat of rams."   I Samuel 15:22

Christians who know this truth and still do not tithe, choose to dishonor God. A tither honors God because this action acknowledges God as their source.

The Financial Curse

"Will a man rob God? Yet you have robbed Me! But you say, 'In what way have we robbed You?' In tithes and offerings. You are cursed with a curse, for you have robbed me, even this whole nation."
Malachi 3:8-9

The Bible declares that Christians who do not tithe are thieves! It is no wonder God says you are cursed financially.

There is no way you will prosper financially as a believer if you are not tithing. Your income will disappear into a bag with holes in it. Your needs will not be met, no matter how hard you work. Praying and fasting will not help! God cannot come to your rescue, no matter how you plead. Anyway, why should He help you when you are essentially stealing from Him?

"'Bring all the tithes into the storehouse, that there may be food in My house, and prove me now in this,' says the Lord of Hosts. 'If I will not open for you the windows of heaven, and pour out for you such blessing, that there will not be room enough to receive it.'"
Malachi 3:10

Notice it says, bring and not send. You ought to come to the storehouse to hear the Word of God and fellowship with the believers. God is trying to insure that you come and bring your tithe with you.

Notice also that God does not say bring 80 percent of your tithe or whatever you can squeeze out, but bring all you owe, your whole tithe! This means you cannot divide your tithe among different ministries either. You should be committed to one local church where you bring your entire tithe. I will later discuss additional giving options where you can give money to other ministries under the offerings category, over and above your required 10%.

If things begin to go wrong for us financially, my wife and I immediately examine our books to see whether there is something we have received and did not tithe on. Why do we do this? Because tithing insures protection on our material possessions, and God says, "Bring all the tithe," (not part of it) "into the storehouse."

The Storehouse Is The Place Where You Are Spiritally Fed And Cared For

Would you have the nerve to eat at a restaurant and then walk out without paying? You intend to pay for your meal, however, but to another restaurant owned by a Christian friend. You cannot do that because, by law, you must pay for the food you have eaten at the place where you ate it. If you wanted to support your Christian friend, you should have eaten at his restaurant.

Christians often apply this same scenario to their spiritual feeding. There are Christians who are spiritually hungry for more of God. They are zealous for the power and reality of the Spirit, and they seek freedom to praise God joyfully and in the Spirit. When they do not receive this in their home church, they slip into another church, which offers these blessings. However, they still tithe to their home church, just because they like the minister or feel sorry for him. If you believe in the minister, get behind him and support his vision with your prayers, time, effort, energy and finances. If you cannot wholeheartedly support him, be honest with him and don't cause division or strife, simply "check out." It is wise for you to go to the church, which feeds and develops you spiritually, and to pay your tithe where you are getting fed.

God commands us to tithe so:

"that there may be food in my house ..."   Malachi 3:10

We are to provide a supply for the maintenance of the Lord's house. The tithe is to sustain the ministers of God and to cover any ministerial expenses, to insure that the Word of God is continuously supplied. Your tithe should not be used for the building fund, the purchase of Christian cassettes, literature given to family members, or the poor.

"Prove me now in this." The word 'prove' may also be accurately translated as test! This is the only place in the Bible where God challenges you to test Him, and it is in connection with money. I realize that the concept of testing God is foreign and may even appear sinful. But it is God who throws down the gauntlet, and initiates the challenge. When God says, 'prove me,' he gives us permission to test this principle by aggressively believing for a return. Some Christians think they are being humble by just giving and leaving it to God. That is not humility, but rather ignorance of God's will. God commanded us to put Him to the test when it comes to tithing. Do not be rebellious, God wants us to test Him so that He may bless us financially and prove that He is faithful to meet our needs.

Testimony by Ben Pieterse—Robbed, Because of a Lack of Knowledge

"As a young working man, I desperately needed a car, but not knowing my rights as a tither, I walked instead of believing God for a car! I could not afford a down payment, but after hearing the message concerning the fact that God wants to provide for me, I exercised my covenant rights and within one month, I received exactly what I had asked God for, my own car!"

"If I will not open the windows of heaven..." This is the same phrase used in Genesis 7:11 to describe what happened during Noah's flood. God opened the windows of heaven, and the fountains of the deep flooded the entire world. God is promising a financial outpouring of the same proportion to the tither.

"'...and pour out for you such blessing that there will not be room enough to receive it. And I will rebuke the devourer for your sakes, so that he will not destroy the fruit of your ground, nor shall the vine fail to bear fruit for you in the field,' says the Lord of hosts."
Malachi 3:10b, 11

Here, God says, "I will rebuke the devourer for your sakes." This is the only place in the Bible where you will find that God is prepared to rebuke Satan, directly, on your behalf. It is an amazing promise of protection offered by our Heavenly Father exclusively to tithers and prayers! In 2 Thessalonians 3:1-3 the Lord promises to guard those who pray, from the evil one. God's direct involvement and willingness to rebuke the devourer, differs from other scripture where we are instructed to resist Satan, who will flee from us. In Malachi and Thessalonians, God promises that He will resist Satan on behalf of the one tithing and praying.

When you tithe, you tithe for protection over your material possessions. God will see to it that the devil does not gain access to your material assets and possessions.

Protection By Tithing

Rupert and Bev Poulton personally experienced God's protection and provision as a result of their faithful tithing.

Rupert had an accident at work. He fell 30 feet and landed on his back. The doctors were amazed that he only had a minor fracture of one vertebra, and put him in the hospital for six weeks to be cautious.

Due to God's miraculous protection, Rupert was back at work within four weeks of his release without a trace of the fracture and the Poulton's were spared many medical bills. They were also given an older Mercedes Benz for only $10.00 a month, and after a year they were told the car was theirs.

God Is Keeping Records

The following New Testament scripture reveals that God keeps an account of a believer's actions.

"So then each of us shall give account of himself to God."

Romans 14:12

This word 'account' is a bookkeeping term referring to the keeping of records. When we stand before God on that awesome day, we will have to give account for the deeds done in our bodies, one of which will be our stewardship of finances.

Yes, we will have to give an account! God keeps records so He can multiply our return to us, based on how much we have given. Some may still argue, "I can't afford to tithe," but I say, "You cannot afford not to tithe," as it protects your material possessions.

The Testimony of John D. Rockefeller, Sr.

"Yes, I tithe, and I would like to tell how it all came about. I had to begin work as a small boy to assist my mother. My first wages amounted to $1.50 per week. The first week after I went to work, I took the $1.50 home to my mother and she held the money in her lap and explained to me that she would be happy if I would give a tenth of it to the Lord. I did, and from that week until this day, I have tithed every dollar God has entrusted to me.

And I want to say, if I had not tithed on the first dollar I made I would not have tithed on the first million dollars I made. Tell your readers to train their children to tithe and they will grow up to be faithful stewards of the Lord."[5]

Mr. Rockefeller is a modern day example of what happens when you tithe from your little and keep on tithing when much comes.

Should a Housewife Tithe?

What should a wife do who earns nothing? This depends greatly on her husband. If he is saved, then as a family unit they should tithe. If her

---

5. Knight's *Master Book of New Illustrations,* Walter B. Knight, page 689

husband is not saved and she is not working, it depends on his perspective on tithing. Many husbands do not mind if their wives give to the church, but if the husband does object, then do not tithe against his will, as it would probably push him further away from his salvation.

Ladies in this situation usually ask if they, therefore, forfeit the tither's reward? I would like to say that God understands the situation and will reward you regardless, but God's Word is very clear. You are either saved or you are not. You are either baptized in water or not, either tithing or not. You do not get rewarded for good intentions. You must tithe!

There is an alternative. You can believe God for seed to sow. You are not limited to your husband's income, since he is not your source. Look to God as your Source and believe for an income, so that you can have seed to sow and tithes to pay. It can be done, and you can also receive the "tither's blessing" by tithing on anything given to you as a gift.

Tithing in the New Testament

Many people are ignorant of the fact that tithing is a New Testament principle. They have the misguided notion that tithing is part of the Mosaic Law, and therefore, an unnecessary practice for New Testament believers. The first reference is found in the book of Hebrews.

"For this Melchizedek, King of Salem, priest of the Most High God, who met Abraham returning from the slaughter of the kings, and blessed him, to whom also Abraham gave a tenth part of all, first being translated 'king of righteousness,' and then also king of Salem, meaning 'king of peace,' without father, without mother, without genealogy, having neither beginning of days nor end of life, but made like the Son of God, remains a priest continually. Now consider how great this man was, to whom even the patriarch Abraham gave a tenth of the spoils. And indeed those who are the sons of Levi, who receive the priesthood, have a commandment to receive tithes from the people according to the law, that is, from their brethren, though they have come from the loins of Abraham; but he whose genealogy is not derived from them received tithes from Abraham and blessed him who had the promises. Now beyond all contradiction the lesser is blessed by the better. Here mortal men receive tithes, but there he receives them, of whom it is witnessed that he lives. Even Levi, who receives tithes, paid tithes through Abraham, so to speak, for he was still in the loins of his father when Melchizedek met him." *Hebrews 7:1-10*

"Here mortal men receive tithes ..." This is present tense. The writer of the book of Hebrews wrote some 35 years after the death and resurrection of Jesus Christ and said: "Here [or now] mortal men are still receiving tithes." The writer is referring to ministers.

The disciples and apostles, who were alive when this letter to the Hebrews was written, were receiving tithes in Jesus' place. Jesus received tithes during His earthly ministry. But now mortal men (in contrast with Jesus) were receiving tithes, after Jesus' ascension.

"...but there he receives them." Who is the "he" referred to by the writer? Melchizedek? No! Melchizedek had died. The last part of the verse says:

"...of whom it is witnessed that he lives." Melchizedek is not alive today but Jesus is. Jesus is the only person this passage could be referring to, since no other person qualifies as living perpetually. Thus, Jesus Christ received tithes and, through His ministers, is still receiving tithes today.

When tithes are given to ministers of the Gospel, they are actually being given to Christ, because He receives and accepts the tithes. The tithe is given to the Lord, but is offered through men of God, as a spiritual act of worship and thanksgiving.

Jesus Endorsed Tithing

> *"'Woe to you, scribes and Pharisees, hypocrites!' For you pay tithe of mint, anise, and cummin, and have neglected the weightier matters of the law: justice and mercy and faith. These you ought to have done, without leaving the others undone.'"*
>
> *Matthew 23:23*

According to Strong's *Exhaustive Concordance of the Bible*, the word 'ought'[6] is the identical Greek word 'must'[7] used in John 3:7. "You must be born again."

If Jesus wanted to change the principle of tithing in the New Testament, He could have done it right here, but He did not! He said they must tithe, as well as observe the weightier matters.

Jesus introduces the concept of paying a tithe rather than giving them. He infers, in the strongest possible language, that we are obligated to pay this portion of our financial assets and income to the church, as the money belongs to God.

---

6. Strong's *Exhaustive Concordance of the Bible*, page 762.
7. Strong's *Exhaustive Concordance of the Bible*, page 702.

Before we study the next New Testament scripture, remember your tithe corresponds to a fixed proportion of your income, ten percent! Furthermore you can only tithe on what you have already received. With this knowledge, let's read on.

"Now concerning the money contributed for [the relief of] the saints (God's people): you are to do the same as I directed the churches of Galatia to do. On the first [day] OF EACH WEEK, let EVERY ONE OF YOU (personally) put aside something and save it up AS HE HAS PROSPERED—in proportion to what he is given so that no collections will need to be taken after I come."

I Corinthians 16:1-2 AMP

"As he has prospered..." is a past tense statement referring to what God has already done for you, and indicates that you have possession of the blessing. "As" refers to the quantity received (in proportion) and, at the same time, includes the thought that everyone had the foreknowledge of what proportion to set aside. "Each week" indicates giving on a regular basis. "Let each one of you," means every person.

According to Barna Research, "Americans were more generous in 2001 than in 2000"[8]. "In total, one out of 12 adults (8%) had given away at least 10% of their income last year. That was marginally above the 6% registered in 2000. The proportion of those tithing is higher among born again Christians (14% tithed) than among non-born again adults (5%)."

Do you know that if everyone in the church tithed, no additional offerings would be necessary? However, at this moment, only 8% of the members of the body of Christ are tithing, which means that 92% are under a financial curse and living in disobedience. Only 8 out of 100 Christians are doing their part in carrying the load of spreading the Gospel to the world. It is no wonder that so many Christians experience financial difficulty. The church, as a result, is also functioning at a fraction of its potential and available material resources.

If the minister says anything to his congregation about their lethargy in tithing, then those in the congregation who are lending their ears to Satan's lies get offended. My advice to such a preacher is, "Keep preaching prosperity until your congregation understands the true message."

I refuse to permit Satan to intimidate me and rob the Body of Christ of their rightful inheritance. After all, this is God's plan for them to be blessed!

---

8. Barna Research, Publihsd findings on line April 9, 2002.

If everyone gave ten percent of their income, there would be an equal commitment amongst the Children of God, and everyone would be supporting the Gospel in proportion to what they have.

What usually happens when the church has a financial need or a special project to complete? The poorer folks think the rich guys ought to take care of it. The rich folks in turn will not do it, as they feel they have earned their money the hard way, and are holding on to it.

To Pastors and traveling ministers I would like to say, do not look to the rich people to support the Gospel. Look to God, and you will find that it is the man in the street, the everyday person who responds. Although they do not have much to give, they are faithful.

It Does Not Pay to Borrow From God

"If a man wants at all to redeem any of his tithes, he shall add one-fifth to it."   *Leviticus 27:31*

The fifth part is twenty percent interest. If you decide to borrow some of your tithe this month because you are a little tight, you are required to pay your normal ten percent the next month, plus what you have borrowed, plus twenty percent interest on what you have borrowed. "Oh, I thought that if I tithe this month and then cannot tithe next month, it would be all right to give whatever I can." That is not a tither! If you tithe every other month, you are not a tither, but a God-robber. Anytime you do not give the whole of your tithe, God will expect you to pay back what you owe, plus twenty percent. A tither tithes on every cent he receives, whether earned or received as a gift.

Athol and Melinda Stark can verify that it does not pay to borrow from God by missing your tithe. They are proud owners of a very successful business because they decided to always be faithful and not to tithe "on-and-off."

From "On-And-Off" To Always On

After years of on-and-off tithing when they felt they could, the Stark's decided to pay tithe first and trust God to help them cover their debt. Immediately they saw God's blessings materialize. They commenced a business and committed it to God as a financial channel. They borrowed the initial investment.

As they continued to faithfully pay their tithe and increase their giving they were tested, they obeyed, and to this day are reaping the return.

Tithing Without a Substantial Return

Many believers have remarked that they tithe with no real outstanding return. After having done a survey on a large cross-section of Christians, including ministers such as myself, I believe this statement is true! Ninety-nine percent of Christians who have been tithing have not experienced an outstanding return!

Do not misunderstand me. Most tithers acknowledge that they have prospered, but none of them have experienced the "windows of heaven being opened" upon them so that there is no room for them to contain their blessings. What is the problem? After much research and prayer about this, I believe this is the answer.

When words appear in the King James Bible in italics, it means that they are not in the original Hebrew or Greek manuscripts, but have been inserted by the translators or the early church fathers for clarity and understanding. With this in mind, let's re-examine Malachi 3:10 and take note of the words printed in capital letters.

> *"'Bring all the tithes into the storehouse, that there may be food in My house, and prove me now in this,' says the Lord of hosts, 'If I will not open for you the windows of heaven and pour out for you SUCH blessing, that THERE will not BE ROOM enough TO RECEIVE IT.'"*　　　　　　　　　　　　　　　*Malachi 3:10*

The words: "such," "there will," "be room," "to receive it" are italicized in the King James Bible. Now, take these words out and read it again as it would have appeared in original form.

> *"If I will not open for you the windows of heaven, and pour out for you a blessing, that is not enough."*

If you tithe, God will "open the windows of heaven and pour you out a blessing that is not enough." What does this mean? In order to answer your question, let me quote verse eight of the same chapter.

> *"Will a man rob God? Yet you have robbed Me! But you say in what have we robbed you? In tithes and offerings."*　　　　*Malachi 3:8*

Notice: "in tithes and offerings," the accusation is that God has been robbed not only in tithes, but also in regard to offerings that have not been given. Why does the Holy Spirit go on and explain tithing but totally ignore offerings, since nothing more is mentioned? That is not the case. In verse 10, God re-introduces the subject of offerings by informing us that the blessings we receive from tithes will not be "enough," and that

ly get a certain part of the job done, namely the protection
. However, to enjoy the overflowing financial return, you
offerings.

in summary, God's financial plan will do two things simultaneously:

A) It will enable the Gospel to be preached throughout the whole world so that multitudes may be saved and grow to maturity.
B) It will cause you (the giver) to prosper and become financially secure.

God's financial plan is carried out through prayers, tithes, and offerings. When you tithe, you say "thank you" to God for His blessings and protection. This chapter focused on the specifics of tithing according to God's Word, and answered questions regarding what is required of the believer. It is your duty and financial responsibility to give 10% of your gross income to support the ministry that feeds you, your home church. The Bible teaches us to give 10% from our capital gains and assets, as well as our monthly income. In turn, this money gives your church the ability to finance the salvation of many. When you give with a willing heart, you tell God that you are fully committed to Him with everything you own, and you acknowledge Him as your source. When you do not give, there is no way for you to prosper financially.

God challenges us to "prove" Him. This is the only place in the Bible where God challenges us to test Him. He in turn promises to bless us financially and faithfully meet all our needs, but only after we test Him by giving sacrificially. Tithing is very much a part of a committed and mature Christian walk. Jesus endorsed tithing time and again, although He had the opportunity to take it out of the new covenant if He had wanted to. We are commanded to give a bare minimum 10% tithe in order to gain God's protection from the devil, over our possessions. To receive the promised overflowing financial return, it is necessary to give offerings over and above the mandatory 10%. These are offerings and will be examined in detail in the following chapters.

Chapter 10

Reach Your Maximum Potential Financially

Beyond the Tithe With Jesus

The Old Testament required obedience to the law, but in the New Testament, believers are required to live by faith. Jesus expects us to tithe in obedience, and then to go further, and give offerings by faith. Once you have received your income and have it in your hand, it is yours to do with as you wish. You may choose to pay your tithe, and be obedient, or you may choose not to, and be disobedient! In this regard, your faith is not tested, but your faithfulness is.

In the giving of offerings, however, your faith is involved, because "seed faith" offerings are given in advance of your return. You plant your seed for a crop, which is still to be harvested. You tithe from income already received!

Dr. Oral Roberts, a man whom I highly respect and admire, coined a phrase, which accurately describes the action of New Testament offerings ~ "seed faith." You are sowing seed by faith, expecting to harvest. If you have not read Dr. Roberts' book, *The Miracle of Seed Faith*, I highly recommend that you do.

You Do Not Qualify For Great Rewards Because You Tithe

*"When you have done all those things which you are commanded,
say, 'We are unprofitable servants. We have only done what was
our duty to do.'"*   Luke 17:10

You have only done your duty when you tithe 10%. This ties in perfectly with Malachi 3:10. God promises to give you a return, but tithing is "not enough" to produce the overtaking blessing. You are an unprofitable servant, since you have only done what was expected of you. Tithing only primes the pump.

You are not entitled to an outstanding reward for expected obedience. Tithing is the minimum requirement, not the maximum. Bear in mind that the Bible already establishes:

"And all the tithe of the land...is the Lord's. It is Holy to the Lord."
Leviticus 27:30

Your tithe does not belong to you--it belongs to God. I like to look at it this way; all that I have and all that I receive, is God's anyway. He says, "Son, I am going to give you 90 percent and I am going to hold back only 10 percent with which to run My Kingdom."

God is doing a far better job of running His Kingdom on ten percent than you and I are doing running our lives on ninety percent. Apply yourself and be diligent with your ninety percent, and stop being so concerned with what God is doing with His ten percent.

Stop trying to be a good steward over God's ten percent. Give it to the Lord and be done with it. Why do you want to tell your Pastor how he must use the tithe? God does not tell you how to handle your portion.

To reach the maximum financial potential, one must give over and above his tithe. This kind of unselfish action generates the highest possible return, since it is a free-will offering.

Local Church or Traveling Ministry

Many believers are confused and, in their ignorance, have split and divided their tithe among a number of different ministries, which they believe merit support. These ministries may well be worthy of support, but this does not change the scriptural instruction to "Bring all the tithes into the storehouse." The storehouse, as we have already found, is the place that feeds and cares for you. Many believers claim they do not receive the teaching they desire from their local church and so they feel at liberty to tithe to TV, radio, tape and mail ministries. This is unscriptural, as no one can receive the essential, and necessary, pastoral care and oversight via the mass media.

If you are a member of a church which insists on preaching it's own traditional doctrines based on man's ideas, rather than boldly proclaiming the New Testament Gospel, then by all means tithe to the ministry which is an alternative source of inspirational teaching for you. The question is, why put your eternal life in jeopardy by remaining in such a church? Instead you should find a New Testament Church. While you are searching for a new home you may also tithe to another ministry.

If you, on the other hand, belong to a good, solid Word church, then your entire tithe should be paid there. Additional offerings may, however, be given to support any other ministry you choose. You may give to any ministry, but only after you have tithed to your home church.

Financial Gifts Are Only Considered Offerings Once You Have Tithed

The following is an example of how not to proceed. Let me give you an example: A man who is earning $3,000 per month, goes to church once per Sunday for four weeks and gives fifty dollars ($50) each Sunday. Has this man tithed, or has he given offerings? He did not tithe because he did not give his whole tenth! He only gave $200 [instead of $300], which does not qualify as the tithe. He also did not give an offering since an offering can only be given after the tithe is fully paid. When you give over and above your tithe, then it is an offering.

Unfortunately, this sincere individual does not understand God's financial plan. All he really did was ease his conscience! This is the major reason why Christians, in general, are not prospering, as they should. Their giving has only eased their consciences because they think that God will be satisfied no matter how much they give. Though I realize these words are harsh, it is important that you know the truth in order to be set free.

Your return is simply a multiple of what you have given. Therefore, you determine the size of your return when you give.

> *"Give, and it will be given to you: good measure, pressed down, shaken together, and running over will be put into your bosom.*
> *For with the same measure that you use, it will be measured back to you."* Luke 6:38

Your tithes "open the windows of heaven" but your offerings determine how much will come through the windows. The measure that you use when giving will be the measure that you receive with. If you give with teaspoons, you will receive in teaspoons. If you give in bucket loads, you will receive in bucket loads. If you only have one dollar and you give that, then you are like the widow woman who gave all she had. This is giving sacrificially, which attracts the highest possible return; this is because you are not giving out of surplus funds. You have given your all and shown your absolute dependence upon God.

> *"It is possible to give away and become richer! It is also possible to hold on too tightly and lose everything. Yes, the liberal man shall be rich! By watering others, he waters himself."*
> Proverbs 11:24, 25 TLB

Is it any wonder why the carnal mind cannot grasp spiritual things? This scripture is totally opposed to the way man thinks.

> *"Cast your bread upon the waters, for you will find it after many days..."*
> Ecclesiastes 11:1

'Bread' is symbolic of that which sustains you, and 'water' throughout scripture symbolizes people. So give that which sustains your life, give your very substance to people, and God says what you give shall come back to you, after many days! Keep giving and it will eventually come back to you on every wave!

Giving to the Poor

When we give to those in need, we lend to God, and the Word declares He will repay us dollar for dollar. Every time you give to the poor, it is recorded as God owing you money, and because God has no debt, He will certainly repay you.

> *"He who has pity on the poor lends to the Lord, and He will pay back what he has given."*
> Proverbs 19:17

Giving to the poor is an important part of the Gospel and we should not shy away from our responsibility. Jesus' instructions to the rich young ruler was based on the truth found in the following scripture:

> *"Blessed is he who considers the poor; the Lord will deliver him in time of trouble. The Lord will preserve and keep him alive, and he will be blessed on the earth."*
> Psalms 41:1-2

Can you see how Jesus was trying to help that rich young man to have a continuous financial supply, and also be protected? Jesus knew that after His ascension, the disciples would need protection, as they preached the Gospel.

Although giving to the poor is vital, you should not fall for every sob story you hear.

A wise person once said, "Give a man a fish and he will eat for one day, but teach him how to fish and he will eat for the rest of his life." Teach a poor man how to fish, how? By teaching him:

1) The Word of God
2) How to apply the Word of God
3) How to receive faith
4) To 'give' his way out of debt

If you do not do this, the poor person will see you as their source of supply, instead of looking to God in faith.

Jackie and I, at one time, owned two successful businesses, largely as a result of giving. We would travel to some of the poorest areas and give them TV sets, VCR's, Christian videos, books and tapes. Then for a whole week we would teach them how to appropriate God's promises in order to raise them out of poverty.

The results were phenomenal. Many people were born again and healed. On one occasion, while ministering at a church, God gave me an instruction and an entire congregation was Spirit-filled simultaneously without me touching them. The Pastors reported that over the ensuing months, many of their congregation members became debt-free as they applied these principles, and the local church became effective for the Kingdom.

In summary, you are to reach your maximum financial potential by tithing 10% in obedience, and then giving further offerings in faith. Your tithe alone does not qualify you for great rewards, because it is expected of you. To get the highest possible return, you must give over and above what is required. You show your absolute dependence upon God when you give sacrificially. You automatically give a full 10% of your entire monthly income to the body that feeds you spiritually. After that gift, you are free to give offerings in as many ways as you wish.

You can contribute to various ministries, struggling relatives, and the poor. When giving to the poor, remember to teach them how to fish rather than just giving them the fish. This enables them to get out of poverty and then help others to do the same. Make sure that they learn to recognize God as their source, rather than forming a dependency upon you. As you continue to follow these principles, the windows of heaven will open for you exponentially.

Chapter 11

Simple Principles That Produce Awesome Results

M
any Christians are not aware that there are specific principles that must be applied when giving, otherwise your return will be hindered or possibly even annihilated. Let's examine the principles found in II Corinthians 9, from the Amplified New Testament.

> *"Now about the offering that is [to be made] for the saints--God's people [in Jerusalem]- it is quite superfluous that I should write you; For I am well acquainted with your willingness-- your readiness and your eagerness to promote it--and I have proudly told about you to the people of Macedonia, saying that Achaia [most of Greece] has been prepared since last year for this contribution, and [consequently] your enthusiasm has stimulated the majority of them."*   *II Corinthians 9:1-2 AMP*

Not only were the Corinthians willing, they were also ready and eager to promote this offering, and prepared themselves for a whole year. Many pastors would disagree with the Apostle Paul's method of receiving an offering by thinking the people would be reluctant and, therefore, stay away if told in advance that the church would be receiving an offering. But Paul tells them of his intention and their enthusiasm stimulates the majority of them to give even more.

> *"Still, I am sending the brethren [on to you], lest our pride in you should be made an empty boast in this particular case, and so that*

you may be all ready, as I told them you would be; Lest, [if any]
Macedonians should come with me and find you unprepared [for
this generosity], we, to say nothing of yourselves, be humiliated for
our being so confident. That is why I thought it necessary to urge
these brethren to go to you before I do, and make arrangements in
advance for this bountiful, promised gift of yours; so that it may
be ready not as an extortion-- wrung out of you--but as a gener-
ous and willing gift."   II Corinthians 9:3-5 AMP

Notice that all were ready to give, not just the wealthy few. Some
people are so tight fisted that, when they hold their money, they squeeze
it so tight, George Washington gets tears in his eyes! Of course, this is a
joke, but unfortunately, some Christians are really stingy. Never the less,
my beef is with ministers who pressure believers to give with out mercy
or scriptural support.

Offerings should never be extorted or wrung out of congregations.
Those who give under pressure will forfeit their return, as they did not
give willingly.

"[Remember] this: he who sows sparingly and grudgingly will also
reap sparingly and grudgingly, and he who sows generously and
that blessings may come to someone, will also reap generously and
with blessings. Let each one [give] as he has made up his own mind
and purposed in his heart, not reluctantly or sorrowfully or under
compulsion, for God loves (that is, He takes pleasure in, prizes
above other things, and is unwilling to abandon or do without)
a cheerful (joyous, prompt-to-do-it) giver--whose heart is in his
giving."   II Corinthians 9:6-7 AMP

It amazes me how long we have overlooked this verse, and asked the
congregation to pray before an offering and let God tell them what to
give!! Most Christians have difficulty hearing God when He does speak
to them on any topic, so why should they now suddenly hear Him clearly
when it comes to giving? On the contrary, they show by their actions that
they are not hearing from God. It could not be God who told you to give
$5, or even a few cents that was of little significance to you. We do not
serve a God who wants our leftovers!

This scripture does not say that God will tell you how much to give,
but that you must decide how much to give! God is not stingy. I do not
think God would tell you to give only one dollar to test your faith. If God
were to tell you how much to give, you had better be ready to give it all!

You should give a generous amount that you have decided upon. (This obviously could not refer to tithing, as we have already discussed, but rather, is talking about offerings.)

Offerings are given over and above your tithe. God does not instruct you on how to distribute the 90% belonging to you, and you may give it as you have purposed in your heart. He exercised no control or authority over this portion. If you decide to give extra, do it joyfully, as a free will offering, and He will reward you.

You do have the option to ask the Holy Spirit to guide you in your giving, not in how much to give, but where to give. Should you decide to give a thousand dollars away and desire your giving to be most effective, then pray. Ask God to direct and show you how to divide and give the money to different ministries or persons. You decide on the amount, and determine your own attitude when you give. The Bible says that you should make up your own mind.

In the first part of II Corinthians 9:7, God tells us not to give sorrowfully or under compulsion, paraphrased, it goes on to say, 'God is unwilling to abandon or do without a cheerful giver whose heart is in his giving.'

I will make the bold statement that, due to our obedience in tithing and offerings, Jackie and I will not die before our time, but live to a ripe old age and fulfill our ministry on earth (as long as we continue to remain faithful to the Word). This is because we are quick and joyous givers. God is unwilling to do without us! Is God willing to do without you? If you cannot give freely and joyfully, my advice is, keep your money because you will need it.

> *"God loves (that is, He takes pleasure in, prizes above other things, and is unwilling to abandon or to do without) a cheerful (joyous, prompt-to-do-it) giver- whose heart is in his giving."*
> *II Corinthians 9:7b* AMP

I know many Christians who are scratching to make a living, battling to survive, praying for God to help them. My dear brother and sister in Christ, if you will heed the principles taught in this book, you will be able to enjoy divine provision, even in the most difficult economic climate. If we live by His Word as "cheerful givers," God will not abandon us.

The word "cheerful" is the Greek word Hilaros[9] from which we derive the English word hilarious. According to Webster, hilarious[10] means

9. Strong's *Exhaustive Concordance of the Bible, Greek Dictionary of the new Testament*, page 37, number 2413
10. Webster's II New Riverside University Dictionary

"boisterously funny." Synonyms are, glad, jolly, joyful, happy and merry.

The church should be full of fun and celebration, especially when we receive an offering. Because giving to the Gospel means the salvation, strengthening and edification of many, what a blessing it is to give, to know you will reap a harvest of finances, and be able to give again. You cannot beat that! So we have something to get excited about!

> *"As is it written, He [the benevolent person] scatters abroad, he gives to the poor; his deeds of justice and goodness and kindness and benevolence will go on and endure forever. And [God] who provides seed for the sower and bread for eating will also provide and multiply your [resources for] sowing, and increase the fruits of your righteousness [which manifests itself in active goodness, kindness, and charity]."*   II Corinthians 9:9-10 AMP

If you are not a sower, God is not obligated to give you seed. If you have no money to give, it is probably because you are not a sower. The scripture says that God gives seed to the sower, to those who are willing to sow. God knows your heart and has seen how you have handled "the little." He knows whether you will be faithful with much. Not only does God provide bread for eating (your sustenance), but He also provides a financial surplus, or seed, for sowing.

God has many channels He could use to get the finances to you and multiply your resources for sowing. Your job is only one channel. Remember, your job is not your source, God is! Multiplying your resources means increasing the channels available, to insure that money comes to you. God is your Multiplier and your Source!

There is a further promise that God will increase the fruit of your righteousness, which will manifest itself in active goodness, kindness and charity.

What are the fruits of righteousness? Every time you get somebody saved, it is a fruit of your righteousness. In fact, any deed done to help others is a fruit of your righteousness. The giver will have much righteous fruit.

> *"Thus you will be enriched in all things and in every way, so that you can be generous [and your generosity as it is] administered by us will bring forth thanksgiving to God."*
>   II Corinthians 9:11 AMP

Your generosity will bring freedom from bondage and result in worship and thanksgiving to God. Notice, Paul says their giving is "administered by us." Once you have given your tithe or offering to a Pastor or Evangelist, you no longer have a say over it. It is now to be administered by the five-fold ministry, who act as God's stewards, to decide how these finances should be used in the most effective way. It is not your concern how your tithe is spent, but rather how you use the remaining ninety percent.

> *"For the service the ministering of this fund renders does not only fully supply what is lacking to the saints [God's people], but it also overflows in many [cries of] thanksgiving to God. Because at [your] standing of the test of this ministry, they will glorify God at your loyalty and obedience to the Gospel of Christ which you confess, as well as for your generous-hearted liberality to them and to all [the other needy ones]."* II Corinthians 9:12-13 AMP

A Financial Ministry

God will pass over a million believers to reach one person who is willing to be a channel. Believe God for a financial ministry, which is a supernatural ministry of giving.

> *"Having then gifts differing according to the grace that is given to us, let us use them: if prophecy, let us prophesy in proportion to our faith; or ministry, let us use it in our ministering; he who teaches, in teaching; he who exhorts in exhortation; he who gives with liberality; he who leads, with diligence; he who shows mercy, with cheerfulness."* Romans 12:6-8

Make sure your motives are pure. Prove yourself to God by being faithful with little, and continue to remain a faithful giver as God gives you much. God is looking for channels. Why don't you become one?

This chapter dealt with specifics on offerings. In order to receive the desired return, money should be given with a willing and generous heart. Determine how much you want to give over and above your 10% tithe, and then ask the Holy Spirit to guide you where to give.

If you sow cheerfully, God will continue to give you more seeds to sow.

He has many channels, besides your job, through which to multiply your resources. He also promises to increase not only your financial situation, but also the fruit of your righteousness. This will manifest itself in active goodness, kindness, and charity from your heart. You will find freedom from bondage, and watch your fruit change people's lives through salvation. Remain a faithful giver and receive the promised blessings that follow as a result.

Chapter 12

You Don't Have To Be Poor Any More

The poor need to escape from poverty and find financial security now, on earth. We know when they get to heaven, there will be abundance, but if they are poor now, it does not help them on earth, to receive abundance in heaven!

We all know that poverty is the inability to pay your way. Many of us have had first-hand experience with poverty, scarcity, and lack. I desire to assist the poor with knowledge that will rescue them. Permit me to reveal God's plan for you to escape from poverty and enjoy financial security.

"And God is able to make all grace [every favor and earthly blessing] come to you in abundance, so that you may always and under all circumstances and whatever the need, be self-sufficient--possessing enough to require no aid or support and furnished in abundance for EVERY good work and charitable donation."

II Corinthians 9:8 AMP

This scripture is one of the most powerfully positive promises in the Bible. This verse alone is sufficient to prove that prosperity is God's will, purpose and plan for you!

Notice that the scripture says, "God is able." However, that does not mean He will. There are conditions attached to God's willingness. God will use His ability on your behalf if you meet the conditions in the preceding verse, specifically, giving cheerfully and not grudgingly. He is: "able to make all grace and favor and every earthly blessing come to you in abundance, that you may always and under all circumstances..." You cannot be more positive than that! "And whatever the need" is the way God supplies. "Be self-sufficient," He promises you will never need to borrow and will always have enough. Not only will you have enough to require no aid or support, you will be supplied in abundance for every good work.

Doesn't your heart go out to some of the worthy ministries who depend upon our giving? Haven't you said, "Oh God, how I would love to do more, to give more but I just do not have anything to give"? Paraphrased, God's promise to you in II Corinthians 9:8, is this:

'It is My plan and purpose for you to have such abundance, you will be able to give to every good work.'

Abundance is the plan of Almighty God!

If the minimum God has promised to do for you, is meet your needs, then just imagine the maximum!

"And My God shall supply all your need according to His riches in glory by Christ Jesus."   Philippians 4:19

This tells me there is the same amount of wealth here on earth as there is in heaven. How could God supply your need according to His riches in heaven? He does not drop it down from heaven. He must have the same resources of riches on the earth as there are in heaven.

Some teach that you must be poor to be spiritual, but that is just not Biblically correct. Nowhere in the Bible will you find that you need to be poor to be spiritual. The teaching that spirituality and poverty are synonymous filtered into the church during the dark ages, when many of the church leaders were, in fact, unsaved and used their positions to manipulate uneducated congregations. You will not find this poverty mentality in the teachings of Jesus. On the other hand, having material wealth is not a sign of spirituality. Otherwise, the world's richest billionaire would be the Pope. This book is not an attempt to equate spirituality with wealth or the lack thereof.

Poverty Oaths

The oath of poverty that is being taken in some denominations cannot be found in the Gospels. These oaths did not originate with Christianity, but came from eastern cults where Buddha initiated this idea.

A Prayer for Poverty

Have you ever prayed the following prayer? "God, I do not want to be rich, I just want to have enough for my family's needs." Have you ever considered that if God answered that prayer, it would limit your ability to be of any practical service for the Kingdom of God? Why would you want to limit the blessings God wants to pour on your life? In fact, instead of being humble, the prayer may well be considered selfish.

Does the scripture not tell us in Romans 12:20; Matthew 25:44-45:

'That, if they are hungry feed them, and if thirsty, give them drink, if naked, clothe them.'

It does say that if a person has a need you should not pray, "Be filled and be warmed and be on your bicycle." (James 2:16 paraphrase) It says to give them something that meets their need! We ought to have enough, not only for ourselves, but also to give to those in need. Praying, "Lord, give me just enough for me," is being selfish and limits your ability to give to others.

As a poor Christian, it is difficult to give and thereby support the spreading of the Gospel. You are unable to support a committed young person to go to Bible School to train for the ministry, and you do not have enough to give to other ministries because you have nothing left over. The answer is to give your way out of being a poor Christian.

A Poor Man's Wisdom is Often Despised

"This wisdom I have also seen under the sun, and it seemed great to me: There was a little city with few men in it; and a great king came against it, and besieged it, and built great snares around it. Now there was found in it a poor wise man, and he by his wisdom delivered the city. Yet no one remembered that same poor man. Then I said: 'Wisdom is better than strength. Nevertheless the poor man's wisdom is despised, and his words are not heard."

Ecclesiastes 9:13-16

We are not supposed to judge a book by its cover, but we do. How many of you who are reading this book would take counsel from beggars? I am sure the answer is, none of you! Even though he may have the "Wisdom of Solomon," his appearance discredits him in your eyes.

As Christians, we are instructed to preach the Gospel to every creature, since we have the wisdom of God, the Word of God, the mind of

Christ, and the truth for eternal life. However, if you go out wearing rags, based on your previous answer to my question, you have proven that few people will listen to you. Why should anyone listen?

If you were so poor that you lived in an abandoned apartment building, owned one suit, which had holes, your shoes had holes in them, you were sick and your only means of transportation was a bicycle that had a flat tire, why should anybody listen to you? Can you imagine being in such a crisis and saying, "You need to be saved, it's wonderful serving Jesus. I'm a testimony to His love and provision!" What kind of witness would that be for the Lord? That person would probably say, "No thank you, I have enough problems of my own!"

Do not misunderstand me. I am not saying that if you are poor you cannot witness for Jesus. What I am saying is that the image you portray to the world around you, of Jesus whom you serve, is important.

We are King's kids, and so we should not act like poor, miserable beggars. Begin to reign and rule as kings and priests in life. Let's stop pleading poverty as Christians. Shake off that religious poverty mentality. God has a prosperous future planned for you.

> *"'For I know the plans that I have for you,' says the Lord. 'They are for good and not for evil, to give you a future and a hope.'"*
> *Jeremiah 29:11 TLB*

A rich sinner can do a lot of sinning. He can throw wild parties, orgies, operate gambling casinos, and if wealthy enough, he could finance drugs, the overthrowing of governments, political instability and a host of other unpleasant things.

A poor saint is very limited in financial ability to help spread the Gospel. One could minister to a few people and pray, but that is where one's ability ends. A rich saint, however, can preach the Gospel in a hundred countries in one night by supporting the Gospel on local, national or satellite TV and reach billions of people. He could support radio ministries, magazines, books, tapes, and the option is endless. A rich saint can do a lot to preach the Gospel to the world.

Poverty is Not Humility

A lot of people have this idea that they are "just a humble Joe" because they are poor! They are wrong because humility is the ability to receive that which you do not deserve. God's grace makes available to you that which you do not deserve. Humility is the ability to receive God's grace.

Next time you see a believer prospering, do not say, "I wonder where he gets his money?" Instead say, "Praise God, what a humble man!" Divine prosperity is received by God's grace, we do not deserve it and therefore, we humbly receive it. Poverty is not a sign of humility but rather a sign of ignorance of God's will.

"By humility and the fear of the Lord are riches, honor and life."
Proverbs 22:4

Every person on the face of the earth is seeking riches, honor, and life but they are searching in the wrong places. The only place you will find them is with God.

Poverty is a Curse

Poverty is neither a blessing in disguise, nor is God trying to teach you something through it. Poverty is a curse, not a blessing. In fact, it is part of the curse of the broken law.

Chapter 28 of Deuteronomy should be read thoroughly to understand the difference between a blessing and a curse. There are sixty-eight verses in this chapter, fourteen of which describe the blessings and fifty-four the curses. God's view of poverty as a curse is clear in the following verse.

"Cursed shall be your basket and your kneading bowl. Cursed shall be the fruit of your body and the produce of your land, the increase of your cattle and the offspring of your flocks."
Deuteronomy 28:17, 18

Thank God we do not have to suffer under the curse of poverty any longer!

"Christ has redeemed us from the curse of the law, having become a curse for us (for it is written, 'Cursed is everyone who hangs on a tree'), that the blessing of Abraham might come upon the Gentiles in Christ Jesus..." *Galatians 3:13, 14a*

The curse of the law included spiritual death, sickness and poverty. Abraham's blessing, better known as Abraham's Covenant with God, simply stated is, "Serve me by faith and I will make you rich." I suggest you read Genesis Chapter 12 in its entirety.

"So he said, 'I am Abraham's servant. The Lord has blessed my master greatly, and he has become great; and He has given him

flocks and herds, silver and gold, male and female servants, and camels and donkeys.'"   *Genesis 24:34-35*

Curse of the Broken Law

The curse of the law was threefold:

1) Poverty
2) Sickness
3) Spiritual Death

Spiritual death is done away with through salvation. When we are born again, we come into right relationship with God the Father through Jesus Christ and thus, spiritual death is dealt with. While you were unsaved, you were spiritually dead, but when you got born again, you became spiritually alive. Just because you are saved does not mean you will never sin again. Sin is the enemy of your salvation. When we are tempted to sin, how do we deal with it? We resist it. Why? Because we have been delivered from it, by the Blood of Jesus.

What about sickness? This is another area in which we have been redeemed.

"...by Whose stripes you were healed."   *I Peter 2:24b*

So, how should we react when sickness attacks? We pray, ask others to pray for us, claim our healing and go to great lengths to get ourselves healed. If necessary the sick should go to the doctor or take medicine. Do whatever is needed in order to get healed, and simply not let Satan steal our health, which cost Jesus so much to give us.

When it comes to poverty, which is the third part of the curse, we say: "Oh no! Poverty is the will of God for me. God knows my weakness and if I get a lot of money, maybe I would stop serving Him. God, in His love, protects me by keeping me poor." What nonsense! If you really believe that, you'd better stop working, because it would be opposing the will of God for you to earn money. Don't forget, the only man who was called the "friend of God" was Abraham, a very rich man! Rich people need not be worldly and ungodly.

If you are concerned about your financial success affecting your relationship with God, remember that prosperity ends as quickly as it starts. If you stop giving and stop being obedient to God's Word, you will lose it.

I believe that our attitude toward poverty should be the same as our attitude toward sickness and sin.

- Resist it
- Rebuke it
- Get it out of your life
- Do not tolerate it

Poverty is NOT the will of God for you!

If you still cannot agree that prosperity is good, at least agree that poverty is bad. If you cannot be pro-prosperity, then at least be anti-poverty.

Those of you who are poor can change your circumstances and escape from poverty. You can become wealthy and enjoy financial abundance if you do it God's way. You will receive it and keep it by giving.

You see, giving by faith will require that you give in your need rather than from your surplus. You sow in advance, even if you have to believe God for seed to sow. You will have to stretch yourself and plant the first seeds!

It is Not the Size of the Gift, but the Size of the God Multiplying the Gift

I have good news for poor folks! You can give your way out of the ghetto because it is God's financial plan for you! This may seem like tough advice, but either the Bible is the Word of God and the Truth, or it is not.

Follow the instruction of the Word, no matter how hard it may seem, and you will win. It is not morally wrong to give in order to get, if your intentions are to give again.

If you do not sow, you cannot reap a harvest!

"The lazy man will not plow because of winter; he will beg during the harvest and have nothing." Proverbs 20:4

You must sow your way out of suffering. Do not be lazy and make a thousand invalid excuses for not sowing.

Put God First and He Will Put You First

Tithing continually reminds us that God is our Source. This may shock you, but the position of your tithe in your budget is the position God holds in your life. If your tithe is at the bottom of your budget, then God holds a low priority in your life. You spend your money on those things that are important to you.

If your tithe is paid last, you probably have said the following: "God, I would like to tithe, but I only have a few dollars left over." Then you will try to justify yourself by saying, "Lord, you know the problems that I face. I am sure you will accept these few dollars as my tithe." NO! GOD WILL NOT!! If you put God at the bottom of your budget, He will put you at the bottom of His budget. Why should God be satisfied with your leftover scraps?

You cannot afford not to tithe! Your excuses for overspending and your inability to afford it are only hurting you. The very reason you are in financial difficulty is because you are not tithing and using a budget. If all the saints adopted your attitude, then who would support the Gospel?

A Way of Life

Until you live to give, you will continually struggle with the concept of financial prosperity. If you interpret the prosperity message as: "My name is Jimmy and I'll take all you gimme," you are sadly mistaken, and it will not work for you. Prosperity is a way of life and it will work for you just as it works for me, if you follow God's direction.

A good geographical example of this principle is the Dead Sea. It is the lowest point on the earth and has no outlets, only inlets. There is no life in the Dead Sea because it is a "taker" and not a "giver." A dialogue was overheard between two members of a church I visited in South America. It illustrates a common mentality that prevents believers from blessing or being blessed.

One day Manuel and Pancho were sitting on the chapel steps, deep in thought, when Manuel turned to Pancho and asked him, "Pancho, that teaching by Dr. Henry about prosperity, do you believe it?" "Yes," replied Pancho. "Oh! Then if you had 100 sheep, would you give 50 of them for the Lord's work?" asked Manuel. "Yes, I would," came Pancho's response. "Ok, so you would give 10 cows if you had 20 cows?" asked Manuel. "Yes, I would," replied Pancho again. Manuel continued, "If you had two pigs, would you give one of them to Him?" Pancho replied in irritation, "Now you have ruined our friendship, Manuel. You know I only have two pigs!"

It is easy to promise to give what you do not have, but God is interested in your two pigs.

Why Do the Ungodly Have Riches?

Do not question why the ungodly have riches! Satan uses this as a trap to draw your attention to the ungodly. Satan says to you, "Look, that guy is not a Christian and he is prospering." This may cause you to think, "Why, if I am the righteousness of God and I seldom do anything wrong, do I not prosper?" You just fell into Satan's trap by doubting the Word of God, which is your source of faith, and instead, focused on your circumstances.

I believe there are certain men, companies and organizations that have become satanic reservoirs, used by Satan to keep finances from the hands of the children of God. I am talking about companies such as; breweries, cigarette companies, drug cartels, and organizations that finance the World Council of Churches, wars and military coups. They pour millions into the promotion of pornographic films and magazines, and strive to keep them afloat at any cost. As Christians, we ought to be supernaturally prosperous, rise out of our debt and change this ungodly situation to possess these finances for the extension of the Kingdom of God.

You Cannot Receive If You Are Coveting

"You lust and do not have, you murder and covet and cannot obtain. You fight and war. Yet you do not have because you do not ask. You ask and do not receive, because you ask amiss, that you may spend it on your pleasures." James 4:2-3

If your heart is filled with the wrong motives, you will never be able to create wealth. Abundance is available to us and God wants us to enjoy all the things He has given us. When you covet after things, you miss the entire reason for prosperity. Never concentrate on what you can get, but rather what you will be able to give once you enjoy abundance.

Be alert to God's instructions and never be bound to your material possessions. Let your material possessions be constantly available to the Gospel. Beware of covetousness because it will prevent you from receiving.

Sometimes it is easier to give when you only have a little. It requires more faith when your $10 offering becomes $1,000. Furthermore, it becomes more difficult to give because you may start to consider all the things you could do with the money.

One day, a man who had prospered greatly under my ministry asked me to pray for him. He said he was having difficulty paying his tithe that had risen from $200 to $2,000 per month. So I prayed, "Lord, reduce this man's income so that he will be happy to tithe again!" He interrupted me and said, "No, don't pray that, I'll be happy to tithe $2,000 per month."

Be very careful that you do not change your attitude or your motives and start becoming attached to your possessions. God warned us to keep a continuous check on our heart's condition.

Do Not Transfer Your Trust

"...if riches increase, do not set your heart on them."

Psalms 62:10b

Let me warn you that if you do drift from God, you will lose your wealth and security. You cannot play games with God and get away with it. Keep your heart set on serving God. To transfer your trust from God as your source and security would be a fatal mistake. Money must always remain your servant, and never become your god.

"He who trusts in his riches will fall..."   *Proverbs 11:28*

Guidelines to Financial Success

As you are obviously serious about correcting or improving your financial status, there are certain practical guidelines, which you will need to implement and apply to your lifestyle. Ignoring the instructions in this chapter will undoubtedly result in failure to realize your maximum potential financially.

Use wisdom in applying these principles and remember that prosperity is progressive, and so is the creation of wealth. You will not start at the top of the ladder, and instantly be giving a "million dollar" offering. You should start where you are and increase your offerings as you prosper, to the place where you can give millions. God will not immediately give you a million dollars to see whether or not you are going to give.

Prosperity is Not a Get-Rich-Quick Scheme — It Is a Total Way of Life!

Most people want to accumulate wealth, but few are prepared to do so using God's principles. If you really want success, then pay the price! Do what it takes to do it God's way.

Work Hard

Lazy people will never succeed. If you are not prepared to work, these principles will be of no benefit to you. They are not given to make the idle rich, but to create wealth for the diligent.

The Apostle Paul worked hard night and day, not only preaching the Gospel, but also making tents to provide for his own needs as well as the needs of his whole evangelical team.

"Or is it only Barnabas and I who have no right to refrain from working?"   I Corinthians 9:6

Paul understood that he could live from the preaching of the Gospel.

"Who ever goes to war at his own expense? Who plants a vineyard and does not eat of its fruit? Or who tends a flock and does not drink of the milk of the flock?"   I Corinthians 9:7-12

In fact, he was inspired by the Holy Spirit to teach us this very truth. However, he did not take advantage of this, as he did not want to be a burden to the young churches, which he had just established.

"If others are partakers of this right over you, are we not even more? Nevertheless we have not used this right, but endure all things lest we hinder the Gospel of Christ." "But I have used none of these things nor have I written these things that it should be done so to me; for it would be better for me to die than that anyone should make my boasting void."   I Corinthians 9:12, 15

No wonder he says,

"If anyone will not work, neither shall he eat."
                    II Thessalonians 3:10

If you will not work, dear brother or sister, do not come crying to the church for handouts! The Bible says, "No work, no eat..." and do not say, "I cannot find work." Even if you have to mow lawns, wash cars, or deliver newspapers, you can find work with the Word of God in one hand, faith in your heart, and the Spirit of God leading you, as your source! If you still cannot find a job, then go create something for yourself to do.

Don't be a "loafer" use your God given ability to be a "gofer." If you don't want to follow these steps, perhaps you are lazy. It is much easier to sponge off other believers, especially if they are givers, than to work.

The Bible says that we are to have nothing to do with the lazy person who will not work.

"For we hear that there are some who walk among you in a disorderly manner, not working at all, but are busybodies. Now those

who are such we command and exhort through our Lord Jesus Christ that they work in quietness and eat their own bread. But as for you, brethren, do not grow weary in doing good. And if anyone does not obey our word in this epistle, note that person and do not keep company with him, that he may be ashamed."

II Thessalonians 3:11-14

Should someone have a genuine reason for being unemployed, the Church should take care of him or her, and help that person look for a new job. Do not continually give handouts to the same poor folks, as you may actually do them a disservice and encourage them to remain in poverty. Rather, teach them the Word and show them how they may raise their standard of living. Give a man a fish and he will eat for a day, but if you teach a man to fish he will eat for the rest of his life.

"He who deals with a slack hand becomes poor, but the hand of the diligent makes rich."   *Proverbs 10:4*

Make "Excellence" Your Motto

If you are not prepared to discipline yourself, you will never be a success at anything. You should operate your entire lifestyle with excellence and diligence in your home, at work and in your spiritual life.

Do everything as unto the Lord. We should not be an embarrassment to the Lord because of the standard of our work. Do not duck and dive from your employer, but rather, do more than is required of you, and you will be promoted sooner than you anticipate. Let your example shine before unbelievers because you are working as unto the Lord.

The First Will be Last

"But many who are first will be last, and the last first."

Mark 10:31

It is intended for those obedient here on earth to receive this promise. Many Christians use it as a religious excuse for failure and suffering, i.e. though they are last on earth, they will be first in heaven. While God does say we will face trials in His name while on earth, He never says we have to be underdogs, suffering always for the cause of Christ, until we reach our eternal promise.

We are already the head and not the tail, we are already above and not beneath, and we are already more than conquerors in Christ.

"Yet in all these things we are more than conquerors through Him who loved us." Romans 8:37

The problem is that we have not realized who we are in Christ. God's divine power has already...

"given us all things that pertain to life and godliness, through the knowledge of Jesus..." II Peter 1-3

Correct your thinking, and realize that you have the authority and are leading the pack, not the sinners. The only reason they have millions is because the church has always thought money was evil and unspiritual, and, that prosperity would cause Christians to forsake Christ. Satan has used this ignorance to hold the Church in fear and poverty, and has robbed them of their blood-bought rights and privileges.

When Mark 10:31 is read in context, it tells us that there is going to be a reversal of financial positions. Jesus is teaching about money, and He says, "Many who are first now, will be last." Glory to God! The wealth of the sinner will be transferred to us. Just watch and see! Remember, you do not have to be poor on earth while you wait for your promised heavenly riches. God wants to bless believers and use them to channel His funds to spread the Gospel. Christians need to get rid of the poverty mentality. God wants to bless you, so do not limit His blessings by asking for just enough for you, that is selfish. Your selfishness will limit not only the personal blessings you will receive, but also the blessings of others that God intended to channel through you.

Don't forget:
- Poverty is a curse of the broken law, and we must recognize it as such.
- The curse of the broken law was poverty, sickness, and spiritual death.
- Our acceptance of salvation, through Christ's death on the cross, wipes out the hold all three of these areas have on our lives.
- Our continued obedience keeps God's protection over us.
- Put God first in your budget, because this reveals where He stands on your priority list.
- The reason you experience financial difficulty is because you are not tithing and using a budget, so change this!

The next logical question we ask is, "Why do the ungodly have riches when they don't tithe?" Remember that Satan also needs outlets to fight

God's kingdom and establish his own on earth. Non-believers have no protection over their finances, but are merely expendable tools for Satan's kingdom. Do not covet these riches, but rather trust God to provide for you. When He does, exercise great caution that you never start becoming attached to your money or possessions. God warns us to keep a continuous check on our heart's condition. If you drift from God, you will lose your security and wealth. Prosperity is not a get-rich-quick scheme, but a way of life. You must be willing to work diligently. Set a standard of excellence, and do more than is required of you. Your example, and the blessings that follow, should help reveal to the church how the poverty mentality holds them back and is an effective tool of Satan.

Chapter 13

If You Already Have Money, Don't Apologize, Enjoy It

The story of the rich young ruler is a message to the rich concerning the handling of finances and the anticipated return on giving. I suggest you read the entire story before we start to analyze it. Read Mark 10:17-31. Let's begin a verse-by-verse study of what Jesus is teaching concerning money in this portion of Scripture.

> *"Now as He (Jesus) was going out on the road, one came running, knelt before Him, and asked Him, 'Good Teacher, what shall I do that I may inherit eternal life?'"*   *Mark 10:17*

The rich young ruler, like other rich people, had a need. He desired eternal life, yet Jesus did not preach the usual salvation message to him, because He knew what the treasure of this young man's heart was. Jesus addressed the real issue, the love of money, which is a challenge for rich and poor alike. People are not offended when you teach true Biblical prosperity. In fact, they honestly want to know the truth, so they can please God and be blessed as an added bonus.

> *"So Jesus said to him, 'Why do you call me good? No one is good but one, that is, God. You know the commandments: Do not commit adultery, Do not murder, Do not steal, Do not bear false witness, Do not defraud, Honor your father and your mother,' And he answered and said to Him, 'Teacher, all these things I have observed from my youth.'"*   *Mark 10:18-20*

This rich young ruler could have been a perfect replacement for Judas Iscariot, who was the treasurer before he betrayed Jesus for money. This rich young man knew the Old Testament, and had observed all its teachings. He was probably rich because he had kept the Old Covenant, which includes tithing. However, his material wealth was incapable of satisfying his spiritual hunger, and he now desired eternal life. Notice, Jesus loved him, and was not trying to offend him.

> *"Then Jesus, looking at him, loved him, and said to him, 'One thing you lack: Go your way, sell whatever you have and give to the poor, and you will have treasure in heaven; and come, take up the cross, and follow Me.'"*   *Mark 10:21*

Wouldn't I love to hear the Lord say to me, "Henry Wolmarans, there is only one thing you lack!" How many of you could say there is only one thing you lack? Jesus turned to this man and said, "Go your way, sell whatever you have and give to the poor."

What was Jesus doing? He was preparing this young man for a full-time ministry. Jesus had asked him to become a full-time disciple and He knew the young man would need finances. Due to the persecution ahead, he would need to be protected, kept alive, and delivered out of trouble.

So Jesus told him to sow seed for his need, give to the poor and, thereby, give God the opportunity to be his source and protector.

> *"Blessed is he who considers the poor; the Lord will deliver him in time of trouble. The Lord will preserve him and keep him alive, and he will be blessed on the earth; You will not deliver him to the will of his enemies."*   *Psalms 41:1-2*

Jesus was paving the way for this rich young ruler to become even more prosperous than he had been, but sadly, he did not see this. He had become religious about his tithe, and had fallen into a traditional rut of self-righteousness. He felt justified in simply paying his tithe, and thereby thought he had already done enough. This allowed his possessions to possess him and blind his mind to the new revelation Jesus was trying to teach him. Jesus wanted to take him beyond the tithe, to giving, which would have produced the greatest return.

Looking back at Mark 10:21, Jesus told the young man to sell what he had, give to the poor, then "follow Me." Unfortunately, the church has also taken its ritualistic pencil and written in behind this statement: 'but

you cannot receive any reward until you get to heaven.' Jesus did not say that, nor does scripture teach that you must wait until you get to heaven to enjoy financial blessings. In reality, Jesus tells us in that same chapter in verse 30, to expect a hundred-fold return, "now in this time."
In verse 21, Jesus called this rich man to be a disciple,

"'Come take up the cross and follow Me.'"

Verse 22 reveals to us that he never responded.

"But he was sad at this word, and went away grieved (sorrowful), for he had great possessions."

It is a tragedy that he is the only person who turned away from the call to be one of the original disciples, all of whom became the first apostles. Every other person whom Jesus called followed Him!

I believe the Holy Spirit is telling us that great possessions had him, rather than him having great possessions! This is why the young man could not follow Jesus; it was not because he had wealth. It was not his money that kept him from being a disciple and following Jesus; it was his dependence on his possessions.

"Then Jesus looked around and said to His disciples, 'How hard it is for those who have riches to enter the kingdom of God!'"
Mark 10:23

Notice, Jesus does not say that a person with riches cannot enter into the kingdom, but that it will be harder for those who possess wealth and keep on holding it. He further clarifies in the following verse.

"And the disciples were astonished at His words. But Jesus answered again and said to them, 'Children, how hard it is for those who trust in riches to enter the kingdom of God!'"   *Mark 10:24*

Why should the disciples be astonished at His words? Peter, James, and John were wealthy men. They owned a fleet of fishing vessels, and suddenly they imagined their salvation was in jeopardy.

Then Jesus reiterated, referring to the rich young ruler, "How hard it is for those who trust in riches..." It was not his money that kept him out of the kingdom, but his misplaced trust in those riches. Putting his trust in his income, wealth, and possessions, kept his heart from trusting the Lord.

> *"It is easier for a camel to go through the eye of a needle than for a*
> *rich man to enter the kingdom of God."*   Mark 10:25

Obviously, it is physically impossible for a camel to go through the eye of an ordinary sewing needle. Yet, Jesus said, "It is easier for a camel to go through the eye of a needle than for a rich man to get into heaven." As a result of this statement it would be easy to conclude, that since it is absolutely impossible for a camel to get through the eye of a needle, it is impossible for a rich man to get into heaven! If you are a prosperous born again Christian, you may be very concerned at this stage. How can it be that you are rich and saved, if Christ Himself said it was impossible?

What Jesus referred to as the 'eye of the needle' was the travelers' gate in the city wall of Jerusalem during His time. This gate would only open after dark when all the other gates were closed, to allow late arrivals to enter. For security reasons, this gate was small and narrow and a camel could pass through, with much difficulty, only after it was unloaded. Once the camel was in, the rider could then bring in his load. This served as a means of protection for the city against an enemy attack after dark.

Jesus is saying that a rich man could come into the kingdom of God, but with much difficulty. The reason being, that all his life he has depended upon his money to satisfy his needs. Jesus is showing this young man that he had to divorce himself from his dependence on riches, give himself to God, walk through the gate alone and accept Jesus Christ as his total source of deliverance and salvation. Once in the kingdom, by faith, he could enjoy his riches again, because he had acknowledged that his security was in Christ, and not in wealth.

Jesus did not say it was impossible for the rich man to get in! He said it was harder for the rich man than the camel. This is because the rich man has to transfer his dependence from riches to Jesus. For the first time, he must exercise faith and trust in a Savior he cannot see. Note his disciples' response!

> *"And they were astonished, saying among themselves, 'Who then*
> *can be saved?'"*   Mark 10:26

They were visibly shaken, suddenly fearing that their wealth might jeopardize their salvation. Certain people who were following Jesus, like Zacchaeus, were very wealthy. (See Luke 19:2–8) Zacchaeus was a publican (a tax collector) who, after committing his life to Jesus, returned what he had stolen fourfold. He could not have returned fourfold unless he was a very wealthy man! The fact that Zacchaeus became a disciple proves that Jesus was not banishing rich followers altogether.

You see the disciples knew they were saved until they thought that Jesus said, "Wealthy people cannot make it into my kingdom." Knowing their thoughts, Jesus immediately put them at ease by explaining that it is those "who trust in their riches" who will have a problem entering the kingdom.

The Deceitfulness of Riches

Well-meaning people often warn us to be careful of the deceitfulness of riches. Are their warnings justifiable?

> *"Now these are the ones sown among thorns; they are the ones who hear the Word, and the cares of this world, the deceitfulness of riches, and the desires for other things entering in choke the Word, and it becomes unfruitful."*   Mark 4:18-19

Riches are deceitful, and they can only offer a false sense of security in which people often put their trust. You make money your god and your source only when you depend on money alone, instead of trusting God's provision.

There is most definitely a deceitfulness attached to money; it entices men to trust it and causes them to stray from their faith. This does not mean we have to be poor, however, heed the warning and avoid falling into the trap.

> *"He who loves silver will not be satisfied with silver; Nor he who loves abundance, with increase ..."*   Ecclesiastes 5:10a

The point here is that money will not satisfy you. If money is all you are striving for, you are missing the entire teaching of this book.

Do Not Apologize For Being Prosperous

God wants His children to enjoy the good life He has provided for them. Any parent expects appreciation for the gifts they give their children. Enjoying the gift can show appreciation.

> *"Because you did not serve the Lord your God with joy and gladness of heart, for the abundance of everything, therefore you shall serve your enemies, whom the Lord will send against you, in hunger, in thirst, in nakedness, and in need of everything; and He will put*

Your Right To Riches

a yoke of iron on your neck until He has destroyed you."
                                              Deuteronomy 28:47, 48

Believers, stop hiding the blessings of God as though you are embarrassed! Your possessions should open a door for you to witness and testify of the goodness of your Heavenly Father.

As a teacher, I share my personal experience with you, not to boast, but rather to give first-hand credibility to God's plan for our provision as I have witnessed it.

"Give and it shall be given to you: good measure, pressed down, shaken together, and running over will be put into your bosom. For with the same measure that you use, it will be measured back to you."   *Luke 6:38*

What I possess is the result of what I have given. We owe it to Jesus not to despise the financial blessings He made available to us through great personal pain and suffering.

A dear friend who helped me write my book "Overcome Procrastination," is a multi-millionaire Christian businessman, internationally known motivational speaker, and drives a gold colored Rolls Royce. One day he was challenged to justify driving such a luxurious car as a Christian. He answered, "It is a result of what I have given to the Gospel!"

The Essence of Life is to Give!

Give of yourself, make giving a lifestyle, and in turn you will enjoy the fullness of living.

"As for the rich in this world, charge them not to be proud and arrogant and contemptuous of others, nor to set their hopes on uncertain riches but on God, who richly and ceaselessly provides us with everything for [our] enjoyment; [Charge them] to do good, to be rich in good works, to be liberal and generous-hearted, ready to share [with others], in this way laying up for themselves [the riches that endure forever] a good foundation for the future, so that they may grasp that which is life indeed."   *I Timothy 6:17-19* AMP

In this scripture rich people are told to give generously of what they have, in order to experience real salvation. "That which is life indeed," and to, "lay up a good foundation for the future." Why would they need a good foundation for the future? Is this referring to their future life in heaven or on earth? It could not be referring to heaven since there will be no devil to deal with, no sickness, and no poverty. There certainly are all those challenges on earth! By giving, you lay up a good foundation and ensure financial security for the future by protecting yourself from the wiles of the devil.

Riches are uncertain. One day you have them, and the next you don't. You will not be concerned about the fluctuations in your finances when they occur, if you have faith in God as your source and provider.

The Wall Street collapse portrays a clear picture of people who depended on and trusted solely in their riches, to the point where they committed suicide when their money was lost. It is the love of money and trust in uncertain riches, which leads men astray. Put your focus on, and trust in, the living God, who "…gives us richly all things to enjoy."

God Gives us Richly All Things To Enjoy

Notice how God promises, and gives to us, an overflowing amount of riches and abundance in, not some, but all things. God certainly does not intend for us to be embarrassed because of His blessings. It is not wrong to feel good about the new car God has given you. A fellow believer should rejoice for you if they see you, rather than label you as unspiritual. Think about how it feels to give someone a gift and never feel appreciated. God gives to us richly and expects us to enjoy and appreciate these gifts. Believers have been so programmed to accept poverty that it takes some convincing on my part to get the point across that God wants you to enjoy the good life! Prosperity and financial security is a fringe benefit of the kingdom of God, intended for you to enjoy.

A Man's Life Consists Not in the Abundance of Things

"Then one from the crowd said to Him, 'Teacher, tell my brother to divide the inheritance with me.' But He said to him, 'Man, who made Me a judge or an arbitrator over you?' And He said to them, 'Take heed and beware of covetousness, for one's life does not consist in the abundance of the things he possesses.'" Luke 12:13-15

Jesus perceived the greediness of these two brothers and seized the opportunity to challenge covetousness. Those who have acquired wealth will agree that their life does not consist of their possessions. For those who are still striving for fame and fortune as their zenith, listen to Jesus' words:

"For what will it profit a man if he gains the whole word, and loses his own soul?" Mark 8:36

Don't Hoard Your Wealth Because of Greediness

"Then He spoke a parable to them, saying: The ground of a certain rich man yielded plentifully. And he thought within himself, saying, 'What shall I do, since I have no room to store my crops?'" Luke 12:16-17

Take note of the personal pronouns in this scripture: "I," "he" and "my." The man was self-centered and concerned only with himself.

"So he said, 'I will do this: I will pull down my barns and build greater, and there I will store all my crops and my goods.'" Luke 12:18

This man kept all his goods, and neither tithed nor gave anything away. He failed to see the importance of continuing to sow, and in robbing God he robbed himself.

"'And I will say to my soul, Soul, you have many goods laid up for many years; take your ease; eat, drink, and be merry.' But God said to him, 'You fool! This night your soul will be required of you; then whose will those things be which you have provided?'" Luke 12:19-20

People often wonder if God took this man's life. God is not the taker, but the giver of life. He is also omnipotent, knowing all things. While God did not take this man's life, He knew it would be lost that night.

When You Tithe, You Tithe For Protection

Because this man did not tithe, he forfeited God's protection. When Satan attacked him, he was vulnerable and lost his life. Jesus called this man a fool, because he was greedy and had hoarded his wealth.

It does not matter how much money you have while you are on this earth, you leave it all behind when you die. It has been said, "Naked you come into this world and naked you leave." Your earthly wealth is useless to you after you have gone to be with the Lord. Put your money to good use now. Plan your will so that your money will be used wisely and continue supporting the Gospel after you leave earth. Why not bequeath a portion of your final estate to your favorite ministries in your will?

"So is he who lays up treasure for himself, and is not rich toward God."
　　　　　　　　　　　　　　　　　　　　　Luke 12:21

A person who hoards up treasure for his own self is selfish and is also not rich toward God. The central theme of this parable is covetousness. This man was greedy and would not give anything, and was therefore not rich toward God. If you desire to be rich toward God, you must of necessity be a giver.

What is the order of your priorities? Is it the following?

1. Jesus
2. Husband/Wife
3. Children
4. Home/Church
5. Job

I believe this is the correct order of priority. Any time this order, or one of these priorities gets out of line, it goes to the top. Be careful not to permit your career to become your number one priority to the neglect of your family and your relationship with Jesus.

"For where your treasure is, there your heart will be also."
　　　　　　　　　　　　　　　　　　　　　Luke 12:34

Your heart's treasure is supposed to be God, not material wealth. Seek God and 'things' will seek you. Remember Jesus said,

"Seek first the kingdom of God, and all these things will be added to you."
　　　　　　　　　　　　　　　　　　　　　Luke 12:31

The following "litmus test" questions will help you realize where you currently stand. If you can answer "NO" to all of them, you have learned to trust God as your source and are on the right track, but if the answer is "YES," money is your master.

- Are you consumed with the pursuit of acquiring material wealth?
- Do your riches control you?
- Are you unable to part with your possessions?
- Are you skipping personal prayer and Bible reading because you are too busy with business?

We know that our God is the King of Kings and the Lord of Lords, the Almighty One who spoke heaven and earth into existence. What about the god of money? Inflation attacks and defeats it. Recently the U.S. stock market turned from a bull to a bear market and 4 trillion dollars was lost in eighteen months. With money as the lowest form of power, are you really going to trust deceitful mammon to solve your problems?

This is the pitfall of many of the wealthy. They see money as their source of power, acceptance in community, and personal confidence, and they put their trust in it. Put your trust in the King of Kings, whose name is Jesus.

There is a solution for you if you realize that money is your god and you want to be free from its' suffocating power. Just give it away! Evaluate the power your possessions have over you, if there is a material possession which is too important to you, and you feel you just could not live without it, get rid of it immediately. It has gripped you, and has possession of you. Yes, this will be painful, but liberating beyond your wildest imagination.

Your Giving to the Gospel is a Barometer of the Depth of Your Relationship with God

The relationship you have with the written Word of God is the relationship, which you have with Jesus. He said,

"If anyone loves Me, he will keep My word…"   John 14:23a

One of His instructions is to "give." Therefore, if you refuse to give, your actions betray your statement of love for Jesus, and reveals that it is not sincere. Your giving is one indication of your spiritual temperature.

Anything that hinders your obedience to the Word, becomes your god. Earthly pleasures, or careers commonly become peoples' gods. Every time you say, "I cannot go to church, because …" you are making that excuse more important to you than serving God. Nothing is more important than loving God with your whole heart. NEVER allow anything to drive a wedge between you and Jesus. Keep Him on the throne of your heart, and put the Word of God first in your life.

Pay Your Taxes

It is deceitful not to pay your taxes. There are legitimate expenses you may deduct from your income before paying taxes, and obviously you should deduct these. Just keep in mind that Satan is a legalist and loves the opportunity to discredit the Gospel by discrediting Christians. When you lie, cheat or steal on your taxes, you are opening the door for Satan to use you to discredit Christianity.

Pay your taxes and believe God for your return! Remember that Jesus said, in Mark 12:17,

"Render to Caesar what is Caesar's."

Doing this is being obedient to the Word, and God said that if you are willing and obedient you will prosper! Every time you pay your taxes, pray for your government, do not criticize it. Pay your taxes with a glad heart and believe that they will be used to bring peace and prosperity to the land.

The Parable of the Prodigal

Apart from the main theme, "Forgiveness for the Repentant Backslider," the parable of the Prodigal Son has a teaching on financial abundance which is seldom, if ever, noticed.

To summarize the parable, the prodigal son leaves home with his inheritance, which he squanders. Desperate times befall him, and he finally repents before God and returns home to repent to his father.

"And the son said to him, 'Father, I have sinned against heaven and in your sight, and am no longer worthy to be called your son."
Luke 15:21

He feels unworthy because of what he has done. He is wearing rags and eating pig slop. He is dirty and smelly. He returns in abject poverty, yet his father runs and kisses the prodigal son. The son says, "Father, I am not worthy to be called your son." His father ignores what he has said. Acknowledging his repentance, the father looks right past his sin and receives him with open arms, just as our Heavenly Father does with us.

"But the father said to his servants, 'Bring out the best robe and put it on him, and put a ring on his hand and sandals on his feet. And bring the fatted calf here and kill it, and let us eat and be merry; for this my son was dead and is alive again; he was lost and is found.' And they began to be merry."
Luke 15:22-24

The father gave his best things to his son. God the Father's heart is being portrayed to us here. When we come to the Father in repentance, He will take His best things and give them to us. The prodigal's father not only met his needs by giving him sandals, but also gave him luxuries such as a ring, the best robe, and the fattened calf.

Now enters the elder brother into the story, which is complaining about his father's gifts to the runaway. There is an elder brother in every church in the world who is always accusing God of showing favoritism and blessing someone else. They interpret this as an act of undeserved love, and miss the principle of grace.

The older brother, who has been faithfully working for his father over the years, comes in from the fields to see that the fattened calf has been killed and a barbecue is taking place! He demands from his father, "What is going on here? You never killed a calf for me so that I could be merry with my friends!" His father answers him:

"...Son you are always with me, and all that I have is yours."
Luke 15:31

The Father is saying to the older brother, "You do not have to be a prodigal son to receive the blessings. Stay in the house because the blessings are already yours. You have whatever you want, whenever you want it. Kill the fattened calf, wear the best robe, put a ring on you finger, because all that I have is yours."

God wants us to have the best, wear the best and eat the best. Why should you settle for something less when you can have God's best?

The Widow Woman

"Now Jesus sat opposite the treasury and saw how the people put money into the treasury. And many who were rich put in much. Then one poor widow came and threw in two mites. So He called His disciples to Him and said to them, 'Assuredly, I say to you that this poor widow has put in more than all those who have given to the treasury; for they all put in out of their abundance, but she out of her poverty put in all that she had, her whole livelihood."
Mark 12:41-44

Many people cannot imagine that Jesus would be interested in money. He clearly was however, because he purposely sat at the temple door right next to treasury so He could see how much each person put in the offering. According to Mark 12:42 (NIV), He saw the widow woman put in two small copper coins worth only a fraction of a penny.

It is also interesting to note, that in contrast with the regular temple attendees, Mark 12:42, in the King James version of the Bible, states that the widow "threw" her money in rather then dropping it in. She may have walked the streets begging for this money, or it could have been an entire days pay. While the others were giving out of their discretionary funds, the widow woman gave out of her need, and gave all that she had.

Discretionary funds are surplus monies in your budget, available to spend on luxuries after your needs have been met. The Holy Spirit asks us to examine our level of giving.

After she threw her money in, Jesus interrupted the proceedings to point her out and proclaim that she had given more than anyone. Jesus wanted to call his disciples attention to the fact that because of the attitude of her heart, her sacrificial giving was worth more than anything given by the rich who gave out of their surplus or abundance. This lesson reveals the giving heart God wants us to have. He gave His all when He gave Jesus as a sacrifice for the sinful world. He held nothing back, and in return gained millions of daughters and sons. Do not hold back from Him. The heart of this message on creating wealth is not how much you give, but how much you keep. The satisfaction and enjoyment of having money is only realized to its maximum when it is spent on righteous acts. You can create wealth for the kingdom of God and for yourself. You can possess wealth and riches, provided they don't possess you. Financial security is a blessing from God and not a trap from Satan, as long as you never transfer your trust from God to your wealth.

Some people are born into wealth. These people should not apologize for a strong financial foundation, but enjoy the ability to make an impact through their giving. If you were born into wealth or you are already wealthy, do not feel guilty when you enjoy what God has given you! The rich young ruler that approached Jesus in Mark 10:17, was seeking eternal life. His sin was not that he was rich, but that he was so attached to his riches that he would not entrust them to Christ, as is stated in Mark 10:21-22. His possessions owned him, making him of no use to the kingdom of God; he was unwilling to part with them. If the young ruler would have trusted God, and stepped out alone, I am convinced that he would have been blessed with even more abundance than he started out with.

Those with riches should examine their hearts and their motives relentlessly. If asked, would you be willing to give up all that you have and follow Christ? While money is deceitful, the believer with a right and guarded heart will not be deceived. Constantly put the Word of God first and allow nothing to get between you and God. Remember the example of the widow who gave all, though she had nothing, and give accordingly.

Chapter 14

You Can't Stop People From Talking

It would be wonderful if believers could prosper and enjoy their God-given blessings without attracting any attention. Unfortunately, Satan does not permit it because he desperately wants to discourage us from pursuing such goals in the Gospel. He thus, brings persecution against us for prospering. Let me illustrate by sharing the success story of my good friends, Derich and Judy De Nysschen.

The Ark Sets Sail

Derich and Judy De Nysschen graduated from my Bible School in Welkom, South Africa, and started a ministry, which focused on the chemically addicted and street people. They started with, as they put it, the "barest necessities: A few blankets, no beds, a small pot and food to last for about ten days."

Pastor Derich and Judy had learned the principles contained in this book, and applied them from the very beginning. They have tithed on every cent and every gift ever received into their ministry, and give away approximately 80% of everything The Ark receives. They are totally dependent upon God to supply all their needs, since their congregation is unable to. As a result, this ministry of compassion has become one of the greatest ministries in South Africa.

They have called their ministry, "The Ark, a place of shelter from the storms of life." It gives life and hope to thousands of people today. Their headquarters is situated in the red light district, at the docks of Durban.

Their ministry is to bring prostitutes off the street, take care of their children, deliver those on drugs and give food and shelter to the street people, the unemployed and the alcoholics. These people are delivered through the Name of Jesus and their salvation is assured through study of the Word. Once this is done, they are re-educated and trained in some skill, to enable them to return to society and live productive lives. Unfortunately, certain groups have spoken about the work in derogatory terms. There has also been unjust litigation against the Ark, and some have even tried to take over the control of the ministry.

Currently there are 30 Arks worldwide feeding, caring for, and ministering the Word to over 30,000 people. If you desire to donate something to The Ark, please contact Henry Wolmarans Ministries for information.

One Hundred Fold Return

I believe the Word emphatically promises a one hundred-fold return on giving, but not without persecution. In context, Mark 10:28 immediately follows, where Jesus has spoken to the rich young ruler about giving his money to the poor and following Him.

> *"Then Peter began to say to Him, 'See we have left all, and followed You.'"*   *Mark 10:28*

The key to the one hundred-fold return is, that they left all. What have you sacrificed for the Gospel? Only the highest level of commitment will produce this result.

> *"So Jesus answered and said, 'Assuredly, I say to you, there is no one who has left (Amplified says: "given up") house or brothers or sisters or father or mother or wife or children or lands, for my sake and the Gospel's...'"*   *Mark 10:29*

In this scripture, Jesus specifies the reason for giving. It was not for the poor or needy in the church, but for His sake and the Gospel's. The sacrifice of homes, family, and lands is not demanded or even expected, but is highly rewarded and honored by God. This sacrifice must be made for the direct furtherance of the Gospel.

> *"...who shall not receive a hundred-fold, now in this time--houses and brothers and sisters and mothers and children and lands, with persecutions--and in the age to come, eternal life."*
>   *Mark 10:30*

One hundred-fold is not 100 percent! 100% of $10 is $10, but a hundred-fold of $10 is $1,000. Jesus said if you give $10 to the Gospel, you can expect $1,000 back. The hundred-fold return should also be understood as the optimal return possible. A good example would be a cattle rancher who gave a cow to his home church. The optimal return could be for one of his cows to produce seven calves in her lifetime.

God continues in this scripture by saying, "now in this time!" Not when you get to heaven, but while you are here on earth! Jesus did not infer that you would get it the next day, but that you will definitely receive a return during your lifetime. When you plant seeds, there is a time period before you can harvest the crop. There are seasons for planting and seasons for reaping. You do not reap the day after you sow. Many incorrectly try to spiritualize this verse by saying that Jesus is talking about salvation when He refers to receiving brothers and sisters and mothers.

I agree that this is true, but "land and houses" cannot be spiritualized in the translation. To make certain that we would not spiritualize this, Jesus qualified Himself by saying, "And in the age to come, eternal life," thereby separating the material from the spiritual.

Persecution for Prosperity

Do you know that when men of God first began to preach righteousness and a personal knowledge of salvation with forgiveness of sins, they were burned at the stake? Religious people shouted, "Blasphemy!" and shipped them out to sea or ran them out of town. It has now become acceptable in some religious circles to have a personal experience with God, but they are still contentious as to whether God heals today, or fills believers with His Holy Spirit with the evidence of speaking in other tongues. The teaching of prosperity attracts great persecution and when you claim that it is God's will for you to prosper, it is certain you will face opposition.

The Bible tells us that with prosperity comes persecution. The good news is that you do not have to allow persecution to effect you. The Bible tells you, in Matthew 5:11-12, to rejoice when you are mistreated, wrongfully judged, and ill spoken of. Remember, you are more than a conqueror in Christ and the Greater One lives in you. People might attack your interpretation of the scriptures as being heresy however, do not let opposition prevent you from entering into God's full provision and blessing.

Pastors are often accused of stealing money from the church when they prosper. This is ugly slander, designed by Satan to discredit their character. Never join the devil's camp by thinking or speaking like this about your pastor or any other minister of the Gospel! Any preacher who applies these principles will prosper! This is not because he is a minister. The same will happen for you, if you meet the conditions. It may be difficult to grasp the idea of a missionary, evangelist or pastor living in abundance, but this is the way that God has planned.

Over the years, humans have become programmed to automatically think someone driving a nice expensive car is a drug dealer, because mostly bad guys own super cars. This is grossly unfair. Many righteous people have obtained prosperity through their diligence and faithfulness. When you see fellow believers driving beautiful cars and living in fine houses, realize they must be faithful givers to God's work. Instead of pointing fingers at other's prosperity, rejoice with them in their blessings, because they must be meeting God's conditions.

When you start to prosper, do not hide your prosperity from people because you are made to feel guilty. Renew your mind to the fact that you are supposed to prosper!

The hundred-fold return is the highest possible return on giving, but it requires the greatest sacrifice and also attracts the greatest persecution. Are you willing to face persecution for the Gospel by boldly proclaiming that God has prospered you because of your giving?

In summary, as a Christian who is blessed financially, the world and fellow believers will scrutinize you closely. I will go into more details about how you should conduct business in the next chapter. In this chapter we focused on how abundance and persecution come hand in hand.

When you plant your crop according to the Word, and reap the promised abundant harvest, you will become a target of Satan. You have overcome the poverty mentality with which he is able to hold many Christians back. This poses a threat to him, as more Christians will follow your example. The Bible tells us that prosperity does come with persecution, but remember, your faithful giving and obedience has also secured God's protection and provision for you. Rejoice when you are persecuted, for you are a threat! Do not try to hide your prosperity out of guilt, for you are supposed to prosper as a result of your obedience. Proclaim that God has blessed you, and be meticulous and honorable in all your financial dealings so that your opponents will not be able to discredit God's blessings upon you. God has prospered you thus far, and as long as you remain obedient, His protection will surround you.

Chapter 15

What Would You Attempt, If Success Were Guaranteed?

S truggling to obtain wealth in the world often gives one ulcers. God's financial blessing does not produce sleepless nights, or anxiety about problems.

"The blessing of the Lord makes one rich, and He adds no sorrow with it."   *Proverbs 10:22*

We have been mentally conditioned, as Christians, to accept poverty as God's will. If meditated on, the following scripture will go a long way to reverse such conditioning.

"Thus says the Lord, your Redeemer, the Holy One of Israel: I am the Lord your God, who teaches you to profit, who leads you by the way you should go."   *Isaiah 48:17*

There is no doubt that it is God who is speaking here. In fact, there are more redemptive names of God used in this one verse than in any other scripture in the entire Bible, and it involves God teaching you to profit.

It is His plan and purpose for you to profit, but many have not recognized it. Alternatively, we have refused to believe what He said: "Give and it will be given to you." God cannot lie! He says what he means, and He means what He says. You are instructed to give so that you can, in turn, receive.

The time has come for you Christian businessmen to stop being embarrassed about earning profits. Stop feeling guilty, because you are in business to make a profit. If you are not, you should get out, because you are headed for bankruptcy.

Some people claim to have God as their partner in business, and very proudly say, "The Lord and I are in this together. This company is dedicated to the Lord!" It always amazes me that God is the Senior Partner, but He never gets to write any checks! God only gets to solve the problems. Even then, men still argue with His wisdom, which says, "Give when you are in financial difficulty." If God is your business partner, let Him also make the financial decisions!

After hearing a sermon on the prevalent sin among Christians of "partial surrender," Malcom and Rhian Rose made God their partner at a time when their business was $75,000 in debt. They owned a clothing store, and felt that they had been guilty of "partial surrender" in the area of finances. They decided to put first things first, according to the following scripture:

> *"Therefore take no thought, saying, 'What shall we eat?' or 'What shall we drink?' or, 'Wherewithal shall we be clothed?' For after all these things do Gentiles seek: for your heavenly Father knoweth that ye have need of all these things. But seek ye first the kingdom of God, and His righteousness; and all these things shall be added unto you."*   *Matthew 6:31-32*

They set a minimum of a tenth aside for the work of the Lord every month, and called it the "Sacred Trust Fund." After twenty-four months of consistent faithful giving, their $75,000 debt was paid off.

Business as a Christian

As a Christian in business, you will be watched and scrutinized at a higher standard than others. Always do a good job and never deliver work, which you are not one hundred percent satisfied with. You must always face your responsibilities and never weasel out of any commitment. Maintain a professional standard and always draw up legal contracts with people. Do not conduct any aspect of business in a loose fashion, especially when dealing with fellow Christians. Upon entering any partnership, draw up a legal partnership agreement to avoid unpleasantness, or even litigation. You never know how some people will react when under financial stress. It is bad business policy to settle negotiations on a spoken word.

An Amazing Experiment

I heard a story about a man named Perry Hayden, who, in 1940, was inspired to perform an experiment after hearing a message preached on the following:

> *"I tell you the truth, unless a kernel of wheat falls to the ground and dies, it remains only a single seed. But if it dies, it produces many seeds."*   John 12:24

This experiment, which became highly publicized all over America, was an attempt to prove that the Law of the Tithe was a divine law of prosperity.

On a 4 x 8 plot of land, Mr. Hayden planted 360 kernels of wheat, which is one cubic inch. To put this in perspective, it takes 2,150 cubic inches to make a bushel. His plan was to then harvest the crop, tithe 10% of the wheat to the Quaker Church, and replant the other 90%. Hayden stated, "In Leviticus 25:3-4, we are told to 'sow the field' for six years and let it rest the seventh, so that is what we plan to do."

He followed the plan in 1941, and drew the interest of Henry Ford, who decided to furnish the land and equipment for harvesting the crop. In 1942 the second crop yielded 55 fold, and again they tithed 10% and replanted the 63 pounds, which were left. By 1943, the acre of land yielded 16 bushels. Hayden said, "Henry Ford himself came out to see the wheat cut, and furnished a reaper to cut it and an old-fashioned thresher, and more land for the fourth crop."

By the summer of 1945, Ford sent a fleet of 40 combines to gather the yield, which ended up being 5,555 bushels. The value of this little crop at the market price of $1.55 per bushel was $8,610.25. The tithe of $861.03 was given to the Friends Church who turned around and gave it to the Tecumseh Hospital.

Hayden talked about the final results, "After Henry Ford turned over a fifth to me, the 5,000 bushels of wheat were sold to approximately 250 farmers in nearby states. They had to agree to plant the wheat, and in 1946, to pay a tithe of their crop to their own church. In the summer of 1946, we expected to harvest $100,000 worth of wheat all from 360 kernels planted six years before, which for five years had been faithfully 'tithed.'" Remember, you tithe for protection, but you give for production. We are now talking about production. Remember where your tithes go? To the storehouse! Your offerings, however, may be given to any Christian or any ministry in need. In fact, no Pastor has the right to dictate where your offerings are to go, provided you are tithing to the storehouse where you are being fed.

There are many successful businessmen who are tithers. You should recognize their names from their popular products. Mr. Colgate, Proctor and Gamble, well-known soap manufacturers, Kerr Mason, inventor of the Kerr Mason Jar, all have set examples by tithing.

J.C. Penny, Inc., is one of the largest chain stores in the world. Mr. J.C. Penny, who went bankrupt on his first attempt, started the company. He later started again, but this time he tithed 10% of his income and continued to increase the proportion given until he was giving 90% and only keeping 10%. On this 10%, he became a multi-millionaire. Tithing works!

I am certain you are now familiar with the instruction to "bring all your tithe," and not a fragmentary part, "to the storehouse." At this stage, I would once again like to draw your attention to Malachi 3:8-9. It says that if you are not obedient in tithes and offerings, you are a God-robber! You will only prosper to a limited degree, because with God, it is all or nothing. Jesus was radical in His life and teachings, and expects His disciples to be likewise.

Do you know that God is absolutely dependent on you to finance and support the ministry you are committed too. If you do not, no one else will.

The smut cartel of this world could care less about the good work we are doing. They would rather pump out the next pornographic movie or magazine. They do not want to give to the Gospel. In fact, they are afraid that if we get enough money, we will stop their ungodly activities.

It is not the unbelievers who are going to help us win the lost to Jesus. We have to do it. God is depending 100% on you and me personally! Do not shirk your responsibilities. If each member in the Body of Christ does their part, by sharing the load and faithfully supporting God's work in their corner of the world, we will win the multitudes to Christ.

What To Do When Business Is Bad

Simon Peter was a businessman, a fisherman who was experiencing tough times. All businesses go through the "no sales" syndrome at one time or another! How can a Christian overcome this bad period? Is God really concerned? In the following story, Jesus solves Simon's business problems. I suggest you apply the same solution to your problem!

> "So it was, as the multitude pressed about Him to hear the Word of God, that He stood by the lake of Gennesaret, and saw two boats

standing by the lake; but the fishermen had gone from them and were washing their nets. Then he got into one of the boats, which was Simon's, and asked him to put out a little from the land. And He sat down and taught the multitudes from the boat. When He had stopped speaking, He said to Simon, 'Launch out into the deep and let down your nets for a catch.'"   Luke 5:1-4

In this incident, Jesus gives Simon instructions on how to obtain his return, as Jesus wanted to bless him for allowing the Gospel to be preached from his boat. Simon had a fishing business but, at this time, his boat was anchored on the shore. Jesus had a need, which the use of Simon's boat could satisfy. So Jesus asked him, "May I use your business for the Gospel?" God also has need of your business for the Gospel!

Just like Simon, even if your boat is empty, Jesus can still use it. Jesus did not ask Simon for a boatload of fish. He wanted Simon to give what he had! Do not wait until your boat is full before you offer help. Give what you have.

"But Simon answered and said to Him, 'Master, we have toiled all night and caught nothing; nevertheless at your word I will let down the net.'"   Luke 5:5

Simon, an experienced fisherman, argues with Jesus that there are no fish, as he had worked hard all the previous night, and caught nothing!

Businessmen today are singing the same song. "The economy is unpredictable." "Sales are tough." "I tried and I could not make it." "I have worked hard but no business is coming in!" You sound just like Simon, with one major difference. Simon did not give up, but instead, he obeyed the instruction of Jesus.

You can make a thousand excuses, but if you will listen to the instructions of Jesus, you will have abundance. Your financial security is not dependent on the state of the economy, but on your obedience to the Word of God. Do as Simon did, and say, "Nevertheless, at Your Word, I will let down the net." Your results will be no different than Simon's.

Sinking Under the Blessings

"And when they had done this, they caught a great number of fish, and their net was breaking. So they signaled to their partners in the other boat to come and help them. And they came and filled both the boats, so that they began to sink."   Luke 5:6-7

Imagine both of Simon's ships were sinking under the blessings, so much business came in that they could not contain it. It is God's way of saying, "Thank you!" Can you see the overwhelming gain for giving to the Gospel? If Jesus did it for one person, He will do it for you as well. Those who disagree, and warn others against prosperity must please explain what happened next.

"When Simon Peter saw it, he fell down at Jesus' knees saying, 'Depart from me, for I am a sinful man, O Lord!"					Luke 5:8

This blows a hole in the theology that teaches that when God blesses you financially, you might turn from Him to serve the devil. Simon was not even saved. The financial blessings that Jesus gave Simon turned him to the Lord. Romans 2:4, tells us that it is the goodness of God, which leads men to repentance, not His anger!

Simon, and his partners James and John, then began to follow Jesus, as His disciples, and left everything to serve Him. They had found the Pearl of Great Price, Jesus Christ, whom is life! No longer did their business, or their wealth, mean anything to them. Their salvation became the most important thing in their lives, and they had to put their priorities in order.

This is what we need to do now, as Jesus still has a need for believers to financially support the Gospel. Offer Him your empty boat, or your five loaves and two fish, and then depend on Jesus for your "hundred-fold return." The amount is unimportant, but the Gospel has need of it! God can feed five thousand with five dollars by multiplying it.

In summary, financial blessings from God do not produce sleepless nights or the normal anxiety usually associated with wealth. Financial success is guaranteed when you do it God's way. This includes:

- Holding yourself to a high standard
- Always facing your responsibilities
- Following through with your commitments

God not only watches your giving patterns and heart condition, but also your stewardship as a worker.

Do not conduct any aspect of business in a loose fashion, especially when dealing with fellow Christians. When business is bad, do as Simon Peter did and let God use your business for the Gospel. Do not let the circumstances around you dictate your trust in God's provision, He will provide for you when the economy slumps, or business is slow. God has need of all that you own, and if you are willing, He will make your business work for His kingdom, even if it looks impossible.

Chapter 16

The Single Greatest Secret
To Increase Financial Rewards

The Law of Genesis is a supernatural law seen in nature, where every tree, every seed, and every fruit produces after its own kind. This is the Law of Sowing and Reaping.

"While the earth remains, seedtime and harvest, and cold and heat, and winter and summer, and day and night shall not cease."

Genesis 8:22

There is a time for sowing and a time for reaping. It is a law! If you sow, you must reap. While the earth exists, this law of nature will continue.

To demonstrate how effective this law is, one only has to answer the following questions. How many seeds must you plant to get one watermelon? Only one! How many seeds do you get back in a single watermelon? Have you ever tried counting the seeds? You will probably not even be able to find them all.

It only takes one seed to grow a watermelon. God's abundant provision, through the Law of Genesis, is seen in the number of seeds that same watermelon returns. Through this example, God demonstrates the hundred-fold return in nature.

Only what you give can be multiplied back to you. Give nothing and you will receive nothing. The law of multiplication is, that you can only reap a multiplication of what you have sown.

God is Not Mocked

"Do not be deceived, God is not mocked; for whatever a man sows,
that he will also reap."   Galatians 6:7

If you sow strife and discord, you will reap strife and discord. If you sow love and friendship, you will reap love and friendship. If you sow money, you will reap money. This may seem a little far-fetched to you, but it is simply the natural Law of Genesis. When you plant carrots, you get carrots, not cabbages.

Can you imagine how upset a hippie would be if he planted marijuana and corn came up in its place? Even worse, what would happen to the farmer who planted wheat, and marijuana grew instead? This is totally impossible because natural laws cannot be broken, and neither can God's Laws.

"For he who sows to flesh will of the flesh reap corruption, but he
who sows to the Spirit will of the Spirit reap everlasting life. And
let us not grow weary while doing good, for in due season we shall
reap if we do not lose heart."   Galatians 6:8-9

There is a season for reaping! The farmer does not plant a crop today and expect to harvest tomorrow. Seeds have to be given the opportunity to germinate. Do as the wise farmer, who chooses his best seed, sows it in order to yield the best crop, and then is patient, and does not give up on the yield.

Sow Your Best Seed

"[Remember] this, he who sows sparingly and grudgingly will also
reap sparingly and grudgingly, and he who sows generously and
that blessings may come to someone, will also reap generously and
with blessings."   II Corinthians 9:6 AMP

This verse deals with quantities and qualities! The quantity you sow is the proportionate quantity you will reap. You cannot sow on one acre of land and expect to reap from ten acres of land. The more you sow, the more you will reap.

The quality of your giving depends on your attitude, and the conditions you attached when giving. Be certain to give cheerfully, without any strings or conditions attached, or your harvest will surely have the same, if not worse, conditions.

Bill was impressed to give his car to a Christian friend who was in desperate need of transportation. Approaching his friend he said, "Joe, I would like to bless you with this car. Simply take over the payments of $400 per month for the next year."

As the payments stretched his budget, Joe could not get too excited about this, but took the car as it was certainly easier than paying for a new one. After a few weeks, Bill received a telephone call from one of his Christian business associates, who said to him, "Bill, I feel led to give you my brand new Mercedes Benz. I have only had it for six months and all you need to do is take over the installments of $2,000 per month!"

As I have said, a farmer never plants bad seed. The quality of the seed is vitally important to the farmer, as his livelihood depends on it. Should he plant bad seed, it is common sense that he will reap a bad crop.

Why is it that Christians give their oldest clothes to missions? We give things we do not need, things that are useless and meaningless to us. Next time an offering is being received, rather than taking out your smallest dollar bill, take out your biggest, and sow that! Start giving your best.

The sacrifices of the Old Testament had to be without a blemish because God would not accept an offering that had a defect. God expected Israel to give their best. When you give your best, as Abraham did when he offered up Isaac, then you can expect God to give His best. Remember this little phrase …"God is your multiplier and your source!"

The single greatest secret to increasing financial rewards is the law of sowing and reaping. This law is exhibited in nature, where every tree, every seed, and every fruit produces after it's own kind, usually in abundance. If the seed or the ground it falls on is bad, it will not reach it's full potential in the harvest. Good seed multiplies itself back, as one seed can produce a fruit with hundreds of seeds.

The same is true with our attitudes and finances. If we sow money, we will reap money. If we sow friendship and love, we will reap friendship and love. If we sow discord and greediness, we will likewise reap discord and greediness. Sow your best seed with a cheerful heart, and then watch as God sows His best back to you.

Chapter 17

Painless Debt Reduction
Methods

We often don't require more money to be free from financial stress, but rather better management of the money we already have.

"Owe no one anything except to love one another..."
Romans 13:8a

Does the phrase, "owe no one anything," mean that believers should have no debt? Many of you are praying, "Dear God, please give Dr. Henry a revelation that we can be in debt." He has not given me any such revelation, but rather He has given me His Word which says, " ...owe no one anything!" I am not going to twist the scripture nor am I prepared to compromise on the Word of God. The answer simply is that believers should not have any debt. Let's have a closer look at this sensitive issue.

"You shall lend to many nations, but you shall not borrow."
Deuteronomy 28:12b

If it were a sin for you to be in debt, or to borrow, then it would be equally sinful for you to lend, because when you lend, you automatically cause someone else to borrow. God would never authorize you to cause someone else to sin. On the contrary, God promises to bless us to the extent that we will be able to lend to others without ever having to borrow.

So, are you living in sin if you are in debt? It is not wrong to borrow on occasion, but it is wrong to live by constantly borrowing. If you borrow as a way of life, constantly living on credit cards, overdraft facilities, term agreements and accounts, etc., and continually borrow from your neighbor, then you need to correct your lifestyle.

Christians are not sinners saved by grace. We were sinners who are saved by grace! We are now the Righteousness of God in Christ Jesus. We are "The Righteous" who sin from time to time. Just because we fall occasionally, does not make us sinners. We do not lose our salvation, and our nature has not changed. Even so, we ought to be living completely free of debt, although from time to time it may be necessary to take advantage of credit facilities. This probably means changing your lifestyle. Strive to be completely debt free!

There is grace for those who are striving to be debt free. Avoid credit cards, easy credit facilities and any term accounts. Do not fall for easy credit or you will soon be overspent each month and end up working just to pay your creditors.

Years ago, interest rates in South Africa on charge accounts rose as high as 25%. Buying on credit meant paying up to 25% more for an item, whereas a cash purchase saved a 10% discount. Based on this scale, the person who bought with cash lived 35% better off, on the same income, than a person who bought on credit. The same principle applies today even though the interest rates have changed.

The person who buys with cash is the only one who has absolute control and authority over their possessions. They do not have to ask for a little extension on their credit to enable them to give to the church building fund, and risk the possibility that the bank will say "no more." Can you really justify your excuse for not being able to give? How does it sound when you say, "Well, God, I honestly wanted to give something to You, but You know what the bank manager said." You have over-extended yourself and are now unable to assist the work of God! You have enjoyed the future pleasures without having the money today. You are crippling your tomorrows because when tomorrow comes, you will be poorer than you are today. You cannot support the Gospel, and someone else is controlling your money. You are no longer the head, but have become the tail.

To be debt free is to have freedom from financial pressures and freedom to give to the Gospel when, and, as you desire. Borrowing is not "sin," but it is also not expedient, as the borrower becomes servant to the lender.

Set yourself the goal to be debt free. List all your debts, and then start paying them off systematically. Choose one account and pay a little extra each month on it. Once it is settled, transfer that monthly installment onto another account and settle it early. Maintain this system until all your debts are paid. Do not open any new accounts, go cash and curtail your spending. Use your faith for a return on your giving, and meditate on the Word. You will soon be debt free.

To escape from poverty and free yourself of debt, begin to give in your need, instead of eating your seed. Keep on sowing as your finances come in. Do not hoard your seed, or spend your money unwisely.

During the Korean War when the Japanese occupied Korea, they stripped the people of their possessions and food. The Koreans had nothing and sank into abject poverty. Their only food was rice, and the Japanese even stole that. One day, a six-year old boy named Paul Yonggi Cho, asked his grandfather, "Why don't we eat the rice that you have hidden in this brown packet when we are all dying of starvation?" His grandfather replied, "Yonggi, that is seed rice. If we eat our seed rice, we will have nothing to plant, and have no hope for the future."

Paul, who has now changed his name to David Yonggi Cho, has become the Pastor of the largest church in the world. At the writing of this book, he has 700,000 members, and still applies this principle that he learned from his grandfather.

A drought-stricken farmer faced a dilemma. He only had seed corn for one season. He could either feed his family or plant a full field. If he plants, he will only go hungry for one season, but if he does not plant he will never have a crop and therefore have no hope of recovery. His decision was to sacrifice for a brief while in order to live in abundance in the future. His crop not only fed his family, but also provided enough seed to plant for the next season. Should he continue this way with future seasons, he would have enough to plant and feed his family, and still sell on the open market.

If you consume all your seed instead of investing some in the Gospel, there is no way you can recover out of your debt. To get out of debt, sow and give your way out! As your income increases, increase your giving pro-rata. Start now with what you have, and correct your lifestyle! Give God an opportunity to get financial help to you. If you do not, you will never enjoy financial security.

Sow in Famine

An amazing incident occurred in Isaac's life during a severe drought and famine. Isaac sowed his seed during this famine and the God-given Law of Genesis came to his aid, providing him with a hundred-fold return in the same year.

*"There was a famine in the land, besides the first famine that was
in the days of Abraham. And Isaac went to Abimelech, king of the
Philistines, in Gerar. Then Isaac sowed in that land, and reaped
in the same year a hundred fold; and the Lord blessed him. The
man began to prosper, and continued prospering until he became
very prosperous; for he had possession of flocks, and possession of
herds, and a great number of servants. So the Philistines envied
him."*   *Genesis 26:1,12-14*

Isaac knew his God, and in spite of the circumstances, he still chose
to believe God. During the famine when no one else sowed, he did, and
reaped so much that he became a very wealthy man! When Isaac left town,
every Philistine stood on the side of the road and said: "How come he
has it all?" They were jealous of his God-given wealth.

Do not only give faithfully in fullness, and nothing when in need,
sow for your need! Sow in famine and reap in recession! If you are experiencing a financial famine and desire to be set free, trust in God's Word
and sow! Believe that the Law of Genesis will produce a hundred-fold
return for you in the same year. Give God a chance to get involved in
your finances.

*"He who observes the wind [and waits for all conditions to be favor-
able] will not sow, and he who regards the clouds will not reap."*
                                                Ecclesiastes 11:4 AMP

Take your eyes off the circumstances, cast aside your fears, and release your faith by acting on the Word and sowing in your famine. For
further information on this topic I recommend that you also read my
book, "Conquer the Fear of Failure."

Beyond Your Ability

Give according to your ability, then give beyond your ability, and
do it all by faith. I want to draw your attention to an amazing portion of
scripture. Amazing because of the attitude of the believers involved, especially when you consider their desperate circumstances.

*"We want to tell you further, brethren, about the grace (the favor and
spiritual blessing) of God which has been evident in the churches
of Macedonia [arousing in them the desire to give alms]; For in
the midst of an ordeal of severe tribulation, their abundance of joy
and their depth of poverty [together] have overflowed in a wealth*

of lavish generosity on their part. For, as I can bear witness, [they gave] according to their ability, yes, and beyond their ability; and [they did it] voluntarily, begging us most insistently for the favor and the fellowship of contributing in this ministration for [the relief and support of] the saints [in Jerusalem].

II Corinthians 8:1-4 AMP

These Corinthians went way beyond their natural ability, and in faith, believed God to get them through the month after giving so much away. Even though they were experiencing severe financial difficulties, the Apostle Paul did not say, "All right, I understand you are poor, you do not have to give."

Many years ago, I ministered along these lines and a poor old widow came to me and said, "Henry! Please pray for me, that I will get an apartment which will meet all my needs." She then opened her purse, turned it upside down and shook out the contents, saying, "I want to sow some faith seed into your ministry." Looking down at the $1.37 in my hands, I choked on my words and wanted to say, "I just cannot take this from you," but immediately the Spirit of God spoke up inside of me told me to take it, lest I rob her of a blessing. I took the money and immediately prayed for her!

In the meantime, my wife Jackie and I decided we would write out a check and give her a hundred-fold return straight away. Instantly the Spirit of God spoke again and said, "She does not need your hundred-fold return, she needs a thousand-fold. That is what I am going to give her so don't you interfere!" She received it three weeks from that day. Remember, those to whom you give will seldom, if ever, be the channel God uses for your return.Giving beyond our ability, by faith, is the way to financial freedom in Christ.

Elijah, in the midst of a nationwide drought, approached a widow who was about to eat her last meal before facing certain starvation with her son, and said to her, "Make the meal and give it to me." Is this a moral thing to do, to take the very last morsel of food out of the mouth of a helpless widow and her starving child? In the natural it may not seem very moral, but the result of her giving to the man of God was a supernatural supply of oil and meal, which never diminished throughout the entire drought.

"Then the word of the Lord came to him, saying, 'Arise, go to Zarephath.' ...And when he came to the gate of the city, indeed a

widow was there gathering sticks. And he called to her and said, 'Please bring me a little water in a cup, that I may drink.' And as she was going to get it, he called to her and said, 'Please bring me a morsel of bread in your hand.' Then she said, 'As the Lord your God lives, I do not have bread, only a handful of flour in a bin, and a little oil in a jar; and see, I am gathering a couple of sticks that I may go in and prepare it for myself and my son, that we may eat it, and die.' And Elijah said to her, 'Do not fear; go and do as you have said, but make me a small cake from it first, and bring it to me; and afterward make some for yourself and your son."

I Kings 17:8, 10-13

Can you believe this man of God? Many people think, "What kind of loving Pastor would say to his starving congregation, 'Give me your last morsel of food and you can have what is left over?"

If you read this without understanding the principles of prosperity, you would certainly wonder at Elijah's actions. The reality was that had this widow not given the meal to the man of God, all three of them would have died! God was utterly dependent upon this widow to keep Elijah alive. Elijah, in turn, used the principles of prosperity to enable God to meet their needs.

You Have to Give First, In Order to Be In a Position to Receive

"For thus says the Lord God of Israel: 'The bin of flour shall not be used up, nor shall the jar of oil run dry, until the day that the Lord sends rain on the earth.' So she went away and did according to the word of Elijah; and she and he and her household ate for many days."

I Kings 17:14-15

God didn't ask her for what she did not have! God asked for what she had, even if it was very little! There may come a time in your life when your spirit will impress on you a need to do something for the Gospel, but your head will logically argue and say, "Oh no! I would never make it if I did that."

It may be that God is trying to bring you into financial freedom. If you do not respond, He will not be able to get the blessings to you. The Holy Spirit prompts your spirit to give in order to bring life, liberty, and financial wealth to you. It may mean having to give all you have, even if it is just a handful of flour and a little oil, one cent, an empty boat, or two fish and five loaves.

Should you refuse to believe, and apply prosperity in your life, you are a selfish person. Whenever there is a need, you will always depend upon someone else to give you a handout instead of being able to help and bless others. True prosperity is not how much you can take for yourself but how much you can give to someone else! This is the message! The more you give the more you receive, and you cannot out-give God!

In summary, there are easy effective ways for you to become debt free, first, set becoming debt free as your goal. List all your debts, and then start paying them off systematically. Choose one account, and pay a little extra each month on it. Once it is settled, transfer that monthly install-ment onto another account, and settle it early. Do not open new accounts, and meanwhile continue to give faithfully. Yes, you should give in your need! Invest in the Gospel, and recover out of your debt. Take your eyes off the circumstances, cast aside your fears, and give when it hurts. God is offering you financial freedom, if you trust Him and respond to His call even in your time of need.

Chapter 18

Eight Quick And Easy Steps To Unlimited Financial Success

The Good Life

Laura Westgate, a housewife applied these principles and as a result her entire family is enjoying the rewards. She was saved in 1983, and for the most part, was unable to tithe because she did not have an income. Two years later, her husband Neal became a Christian and together they searched God's Word to learn to fulfill God's covenant with their money.

They became cheerful tithers, and did not miss an opportunity for offerings either. They were soon able to purchase their own house and received enough money for remodeling and a pool. Laura remembers, "As we meditated on God's Word concerning financial prosperity, it became heart knowledge and we started confessing His Word. The windows of heaven opened and started pouring out God's blessings upon our lives."

The Westgate's then attended my Bible school and made God their number one priority. Within four years Neal had two promotions until he was the #2 man at the mines where he worked, and he was frequently shown extraordinary favor. He now is the mine manager.

Laura continued, "God has given us wisdom to deal wisely in all the affairs of life, making the right decisions at the right time and above all, we recognize Him as "our source and protection in our lives." Laura and her two sons were cleaning the swimming pool, and unwittingly added a cup of chlorine to a bucket of acid, causing a tremendous chlorine gas explosion. It was so intensive that it completely burned and destroyed the flowers 15 feet away. Even though they inhaled some of the poisonous gas they were completely protected.

Harvesting

Harvesting is something you must do continually; just as giving is a way of life. Here are eight Lifestyle Principles to establish in order to receive.

> Principle #1 - Tithe on everything you receive.
> Principle #2 - Give offerings over and above your tithe. Sow seeds for your future harvest.
> Principle #3 - Aggressively use your faith and believe for your return.
> Principle #4 - Command Satan to release your finances.
> Principle #5 - Commission the angels to bring your return to you.
> Principle #6 - Meditate on, and confess the promises in the scripture relevant to financial abundance.
> Principle #7 - Praise and thank God, acknowledging Him for your prosperity and financial security.
> Principle #8 - Be patient.

Since we have discussed the first two Lifestyle Principles mentioned above in great detail in chapters nine and ten, let us begin at Principle Three.

Principle Three: Aggressively Use Your Faith

Believe for a return. You should expect to receive; expect a financial miracle when you give. When someone gives you something, you should take their hand, thank them for the gift and immediately pray the prayer of faith, thanking the Lord for their return as a result of their gift to you.

Remember, you must give expecting to receive. Many Christians are not prepared to use their faith for their return because they believe it is sacrilege to expect God to return their goodness to them! I say a thousand times no! Jesus Himself said, "Give and it shall be given to you…"

You must expect a financial miracle every day, and look excitedly for your return. God is your source. Never look to man to be your source.

What would you think of a farmer who sowed his land and never expected to reap the crop, but just sat in the sun during harvest, smoking his pipe saying, "I just plant and leave the rest to the Lord!"

The compassion, love and mercy of God are limitless, but a "pity party" never attracts His attention. God is not moved by needs. No matter how bad your financial crisis is you will never get God to feel sorry for you. God has given us everything in Jesus. He is no longer moved by your needs, but is now moved by your faith. Jesus Himself said in Matthew 9:29:

"Be it done to you according to your faith."

Notice he did not say, "according to your needs." You have to aggressively exercise faith for your return.

Giving demonstrates your level of faith. You must exercise active faith to prosper and receive your return. We owe it to the Lord Jesus Christ not to waste that, which has cost Him so much to give. He paid an extremely high price for us to have wealth, by becoming poor so that we may be rich.

While you are waiting for your return, do not multiply your doubts with negative thoughts, but rather multiply your faith! Your thoughts create the environment in which God must work, so make certain your thoughts are faith thoughts. Do not be discouraged by the economic drought around you, because it has nothing to do with your return. Your increase is dependent on God, and He responds to your faith.

Principle Four: Command Satan to Release Your Finances

Satan is also called the "Resister." He will resist your return to try to prevent you from prospering. If he can keep you in lack he can limit your effectiveness for the Kingdom. Any part of your return that you don't receive, Satan has stolen. You need to do something about Satan. God says:

"And I will rebuke the devourer..."   Malachi 3:11

If God rebukes the devourer so should we. We have a right to rebuke and stop him from devouring our return. Come against him as follows:

'Satan, I command you to stop your maneuvers to devour my return. I will not permit you to harass or resist my return! In the name of Jesus, I bind your powers according to Matthew 18:18 and charge you to immediately release my money, which you are holding back.'

Principle Five: Commission the Angels to Go Out and Bring Your Money In

By speaking the Word of God, you can commission the angels to go out and bring in your money. We can briefly examine the following scripture, which refers to the ministry of angels.

> *"But to which of the angels has He ever said: 'Sit at my right hand, till I make your enemies your footstool?' Are they not all minister-ing spirits sent forth to minister for those who will inherit salva-tion?"*   Hebrews 1:13-14

The angels are not ministering to them, but ministering for them. The angels respond to the voice of the Word of God! When you speak out God's Word, you release the angels by faith, and they go out and do the Word. God has already sent the angels forth into the earth to help us and to minister for us. Do not command the angels, but rather commis-sion them with the Word for a particular task.

Principle Six: Continually Meditate in and Confess the Promises of God Relevant to Prosperity

Positive confession is a powerful thing, and is often underutilized by Christians today. Just remember, what you say is what you get!

> *"For assuredly, I say to you, whoever says to this mountain, 'Be re-moved and be cast into the sea,' and does not doubt in his heart, but believes that those things he says will be done, come to pass, he will have whatever he says."*   Mark 11:23

Call in your return! Speak to your money and say:
'Money, come to me in abundance, I call abundance and no lack, in the Name of Jesus!'
Speak to your bills and command them to be paid! Call those things which "be not as though they are." Just as it says in Romans 4:11 (KJV)
Never speak negatively, saying, "It is not working, where is my re-turn?" Neve___ Satan the right to rob you through your own words.
___d give God a chance. Say, 'Because I have given, it is ___e, good measure, pressed down and shaken together, ___osom!'

Principle Seven: Praise and Thank God, Acknowledging Him for Your Prosperity

Praise and thank God for your increase in wealth, especially if you have not seen the manifestation. This is the highest expression of your faith.

Principle Eight: Patience

Patience is required to receive, as this is not a get-rich-quick scheme, but the plan God has for you to become financially secure and successful. Do not doubt, become discouraged or be double-minded. It will keep you from receiving.

> *"Therefore do not cast away your confidence, which has great reward. For you have need of endurance (patience), so that after you have done the will of God, you may receive the promise."*
>
> *Hebrews 10:35-36*

> *"Cast your bread upon the waters, for you will find it after many days."*
>
> *Ecclesiastes 11:1*

Where Does Your Return Come From?

> *"Give, and it shall be given unto you; good measure, pressed down, and shaken together, and running over, shall men give into your bosom. For with the same measure that ye mete withal it shall be measured to you again."*
>
> *Luke 6:38 KJV*

> *" ...and prove Me now in this, says the Lord of hosts, if I will not open for you the windows of heaven and pour out for you such blessing that there will not be room enough to receive it."*
>
> *Malachi 3:10b*

Men will be the channels for your return of seed-faith giving, but God will give you the return on tithing. I once asked, "Lord, how are you going to get it down from heaven to me?" The Lord reminded me of the many financial miracles, which had taken place and of how my assets had grown. I had not received from men giving into my bosom, but from God blessing me through men.

Things like promotions at work, increased sales, large commissions, better opportunities, increased value of real estate and other assets, is not man giving into your bosom, it is God! This is the tither's return. God ensures that your interests and material are protected, and that your assets grow in value.

In order to assist you in harvesting your return I have made you aware of Satan's tactics to resist it coming in. He is referred to in scripture as the "god of this world's system." Satan allows large amounts of money to flow into the hands of his children to keep it from us because he knows we will use it for the Gospel. He has created "Satanic reservoirs" which are controlled by him and in which he hoards the money. I have good news for you. These reservoirs are to be drained of their finances by the righteous who will use it to spread the Gospel!

> *"A good man leaves an inheritance to his children's children, but the wealth of the sinner is stored up for the righteous."*
>
> *Proverbs 13:22*

Our wealth will come from the hands of the sinners.

> *"For God gives wisdom and knowledge and joy to a man who is good in His sight; But to the sinner He gives the work of gathering and collecting, that He may give to him who is good before God ..."*
>
> *Ecclesiastes 2:26a*

It is hard to imagine that all these sinners are working for you, and you do not even know it! God has them groveling and sweating to accumulate riches so they can be given to you, because only the righteous are good in his sight.

> *"This is the portion of a wicked man with God, and the heritage of oppressors, received from the Almighty: If his children are multiplied, it is for the sword; and his offspring shall not be satisfied with bread. Those who survive him shall be buried in death, and their widows shall not weep. Though he heaps up silver like dust, and piles up clothing like clay- he may pile it up, but the just will wear it, and the innocent will divide the silver."*   *Job 27:13-17*

The wicked man can work until he comes to a standstill, but all he is doing is heaping it up for you and me. If only they knew how vain it is to seek riches and wealth, without seeking God.

When Will We Enjoy This Transfer of Wealth?

James gives us the answer:

> *"Come now, you rich [people], weep aloud and lament over the miseries-- the woes--that are surely coming upon you. Your abundant wealth has rotted and is ruined and your [many] garments have become moth-eaten. Your gold and silver are completely rusted through, and their rust will be testimony against you and it will devour your flesh as if it were fire. You have heaped together treasure for the last days."*
> *James 5:1-3 AMP*

The prophet Joel prophesied (Joel 2:28) that in the last days we would see the outpouring of the Holy Spirit, which occurred in Acts chapters one and two. We are living in the last days right now! The unjust are heaping up our finances for us to use in these days, according to James 5:3.

Alternatively — Consider Your Ways

If you think you have complied with all the instructions given in this book, and there is still no manifestation on your giving, then consider your ways!

> *"Now therefore, thus says the Lord of hosts: 'Consider your ways! You have sown much, and bring in little; You eat, but do not have enough; You drink, but you are not filled with drink; You clothe yourselves, but no one is warm; And he who earns wages, earns wages to put into a bag with holes.'"*
> *Haggai 1:5-6*

"Consider your ways." I am not suggesting you become introspective and find fault with yourself, but rather that you make certain you are living a life which is pleasing to God. Stay free from sin, and consider your ways!

Do not allow disobedience to steal the benefits of abundance from you. Read this book again! Make certain you apply these principles diligently, and you will create wealth for yourself and for the Kingdom of God.

In summary, there are eight quick and easy principles to unlimited financial success that I have covered in this book. Make them a part of your lifestyle, and you will be rewarded:

Tithe a minimum of 10% out of *everything* you receive, to secure God's protection, and be obedient. Give offerings over and above your tithe in order to open up the heavens of God's abundance in your financial situation. Do not be afraid to aggressively use your faith and believe for your return. God charges us to apply our faith by giving with the expectation of receiving. Command Satan to release your finances, as he will attempt to prevent you from prospering. Commission angels to go out and bring in your money, as they respond to the Word of God and your commission for help. Positively confess the promises of God over all aspects of your finances from the paying of bills, to the receipt of your return. Acknowledge God for your prosperity; that is the highest expression of your faith. There is no guarantee on God's timing, so be patient and trust that your return will come at the best time.

Men may be channels for your return of seed-faith giving, but God will give you the return on tithing. Our wealth will come from the hands of sinners who seek riches and wealth without seeking God. If you are still not seeing a manifestation, consider your ways. Examine your life to make sure your actions are pleasing to God. Continue to be obedient and free from sin, as you expect your rightful inheritance and God-given riches!

Index

H

harvest
  harvested, harvesting 35, 36, 50,
    63, 72, 105, 106, 109, 114, 115,
    126, 127
healed
  heals, healing 14, 16, 24, 25, 67, 80
health
  healthy 14, 15, 16, 24, 26, 27, 80
heart 16, 30, 33, 41, 42, 62, 70, 71, 72,
    73, 74, 76, 83, 84, 85, 88, 89,
    91, 93, 97, 98, 99, 101, 112, 114,
    115, 125
heaven 19, 22, 24, 26, 27, 37, 43, 47, 51,
    53, 55, 61, 65, 67, 75, 76, 86, 90,
    91, 92, 95, 97, 105, 125, 129
heritage 23, 130
Holy Spirit 17, 18, 21, 38, 39, 42, 44,
    52, 61, 71, 73, 85, 91, 101, 105,
    122, 131
home
  houses 15, 26, 36, 51, 54, 56, 62, 65,
    86, 99, 105
honor 22, 42, 44, 79
hope 78, 103, 119
humble
  humility 7, 43, 54, 77, 78
hundred-fold return 104
hungry
  hunger 17, 54, 119
hypocrites 50, 58

I

income 18, 33, 49, 50, 51, 52, 53, 57, 58,
    59, 60, 62, 63, 67, 83, 91, 98, 110,
    118, 119, 125
increase 23, 39, 44, 60, 72, 74, 79, 84,
    93, 110, 119, 127, 129
inflation 22, 97
inheritance 23, 25, 59, 95, 99, 130, 132
invest 39

J

jar of oil 122
Jesus 13, 14, 16, 17, 18, 19, 21, 22, 24, 25,
    26, 27, 29, 35, 37, 38, 43, 50, 51,
    52, 58, 62, 63, 66, 76, 78, 80, 86,
    87, 89, 90, 91, 92, 93, 94, 95, 96,
    97, 98, 99, 100, 101, 104, 105,
    110, 111, 112, 118, 126, 127, 128
Judas Iscariot 19, 90

K

Kingdom 14, 17, 23, 46, 64, 67, 77, 83,
    127, 131
knowledge 52, 59, 75, 87, 105, 125, 130

L

lack 21, 30, 33, 41, 44, 50, 75, 76, 90,
    127, 128
Law of Genesis 113, 114, 119, 120
Law of Sowing and Reaping 113
lazy 81, 85
lend 23, 66, 117
limit
  limitless 33, 52, 77, 87, 127
Lord 14, 17, 21, 22, 23, 24, 26, 29, 30,
    31, 32, 33, 39, 41, 42, 43, 50, 52,
    53, 54, 55, 56, 58, 61, 64, 66, 77,
    78, 82, 83, 86, 91, 93, 96, 107,
    108, 112, 120, 121, 126, 127, 129,
    131
love 15, 22, 25, 26, 36, 38, 46, 76, 78,
    80, 89, 90, 95, 98, 100, 114, 115,
    117, 127
loyal 38
lust
  lusts 46, 83

M

mammon 37, 38, 52, 98
Marriage
  marriages 15

Notes

Notes

Notes

If you enjoyed this book and would like to pass one on to someone else, please check with your local bookstore, online bookseller, or use this form:

Name_____

Address _____

City _____ State_____ Zip_____

Please send me:

_____ copies of *Your Rights to Riches* at $14.99 $ _____

California residents please add sales tax $ _____

Shipping*: $4.00 for the first copy and $2.00
for each additional copy $ _____

Total enclosed $ _____

Send order to:

Tsaba House
2252 12th Street
Reedley, CA 93654
or visit our website at www.TsabaHouse.com

For more than 5 copies, please contact the publisher for multiple copy rates.

*International shipping costs extra. If shipping to a destination outside the United States, please contact the publisher for rates to your location.